IMAGES OF WAR

THE RUSSIAN REVOLUTION

World War to Civil War, 1917–1921

The transition from a world war to a civil war required a delicate sense of balance for most participants. Not every officer supported the anti-Bolsheviks, nor did every ordinary serviceman support the revolutionaries.

IMAGES OF WAR

THE RUSSIAN REVOLUTION

World War to Civil War, 1917–1921

RARE PHOTOGRAPHS FROM WARTIME ARCHIVES

Nik Cornish

Pen & Sword
MILITARY

First published in Great Britain in 2012 by
PEN & SWORD MILITARY
an imprint of
Pen & Sword Books Ltd,
47 Church Street,
Barnsley,
South Yorkshire
S70 2AS

ISBN 978 1 84884 375 2

A CIP record for this book is available from the British Library.

Typeset by Chic Media Limited.

Printed and bound by CPI Group (UK) Ltd, Croydon, CR0 4YY.

Pen & Sword Books Ltd incorporates the Imprints of
Pen & Sword Aviation, Pen & Sword Family History, Pen & Sword Maritime, Pen & Sword Military, Pen & Sword Discovery, Wharncliffe Local History, Wharncliffe True Crime, Wharncliffe Transport, Pen & Sword Select, Pen & Sword Military Classics, Leo Cooper, The Praetorian Press, Remember When, Seaforth Publishing and Frontline Publishing.

For a complete list of Pen & Sword titles please contact
Pen & Sword Books Limited
47 Church Street, Barnsley, South Yorkshire, S70 2AS, England
E-mail: enquiries@pen-and-sword.co.uk
Website: www.pen-and-sword.co.uk

Contents

Acknowledgements and Photographic sources

As ever my thanks are extended to Dmitri Belanovsky who had family on both sides of the political divide and never hesitates to provide lucid commentary on the text and captions. Further thanks are due to Norbert Hofer, Andrei Simonov and Stephen Perry.

This book is dedicated to Dorothy (my mum), Angie (partner and RCW 'widow') and Alex, Charlotte and James – daddy's little soldiers! And to a veteran, the late Nicholas Volkov-Mouromtsov (United Cuirassier Regiment, Volunteer Army), who encouraged my interest in this period and August G. Blume, a deeply missed friend and inspiration of many years.

Images are taken from the following sources:

From the Fonds of the RGAKFD in Krasnogorsk: pp. 13 (top), 13 (bottom), 27, 31 (top), 38 (top), 40 (top), 42 (bottom), 45 (top), 54 (bottom), 56 (top), 58 (top), 58 (bottom), 59 (top), 78 (bottom), 80, 81 (bottom), 83 (top left), 83 (bottom), 95 (top), 97 (bottom), 98 (bottom), 99 (top), 99 (bottom), 100 (bottom), 102 (bottom), 107, 108 (top), 108 (bottom), 109 (top), 109 (bottom), 110 (top), 111 (bottom), 112 (top), 113 (bottom), 114 (top), 116 (top), 116 (bottom), 121 (top), 122, 123 (top), 124 (top), 125 (top), 126 (top), 127 (bottom), 129 (top), 129 (bottom), 130 (bottom), 137 (bottom), 138 (bottom), 139 (top), 139 (bottom), 140 (bottom), 143 (top).

Courtesy of the Central Museum of the Armed Forces Moscow: pp. 14 (top), 15, 21, 22, 23 (top), 23 (bottom), 24, 25, 26 (bottom), 29 (bottom), 30 (top left), 30 (top right), 30 (bottom), 31 (bottom), 32 (bottom), 38 (bottom), 39 (top right), 40 (bottom), 44 (top), 46 (top), 46 (bottom), 56 (bottom), 57 (top), 57 (bottom), 59 (bottom), 73 (top), 79, 81 (top), 85 (top), 86 (top), 87 (bottom), 98 (top), 100 (top), 110 (bottom), 111 (top), 112 (bottom), 113 (top), 115 (top), 115 (bottom), 124 (bottom), 125 (bottom), 127 (top), 128 (top), 128 (bottom), 130 (top), 137 (top), 141 (top), 141 (bottom), 142 (top), 143, 144 (bottom).

From the Andrei Simonov Collection: pp. 32 (top), 50, 52 (bottom), 53 (top left), 53 (bottom), 54 (top), 55 (top), 55 (bottom), 64, 65, 74, 96 (bottom).

Nik Cornish at Stavka: pp. 14 (bottom), 16, 26 (top), 27 (top), 27 (bottom), 29 (top), 37, 39 (top left), 39 (bottom), 41 (top), 41 (bottom), 42 (top), 43 (top), 43 (bottom), 44 (bottom), 45 (bottom), 51, 52 (top), 53 (top right), 60, 66 (top), 66 (bottom), 67, 68 (top), 68 (bottom), 69 (top), 69 (bottom), 70 (top), 70 (bottom), 71, 72 (top), 72 (bottom), 73 (bottom), 78 (top), 82 (top), 82 (bottom), 83 (top right), 84 (top), 84 (bottom), 85 (bottom), 86 (bottom), 87 (top), 88, 92, 93, 94 (top), 94 (bottom), 95 (bottom), 96 (top), 97 (top), 101 (top), 101 (bottom), 102 (top), 114 (bottom left), 114 (bottom right), 120, 121 (bottom), 123 (bottom), 126 (bottom), 136 (top), 136 (bottom), 138 (top), 140 (top), 142 (bottom), 144 (top).

Preface

The purpose of this book is to give the general reader of history, military or otherwise, a heavily illustrated overview of the events, personalities and places that came together to compose the Russian revolutions and subsequent civil war during the period 1917–1921. As my starting point I have taken the abdication of Nicholas II Romanov and ended with the Kronstadt Uprising in 1921. I have no particular political axe to grind in this matter having spoken to and discussed the matter with veterans that had both anti- and pro-communist sympathies, all of whom expressed the common goal of having the improvement of Russia as their guiding principle. Sadly, all are now deceased but I hope, from the notes I took during our conversations, to help others make some sense of the brutal, fratricidal lunacy that engulfed one-sixth of the world's land mass and involved over 150 million people.

I apologize in advance for what some may perceive as an over-simplistic approach to the tangled politics of this period but exonerate myself by the need to condense billions of words into less than 25,000.

The images are mainly drawn from Russian archives, particularly that of the Central Museum of the Armed Forces, Moscow to which I owe a great debt of gratitude for many years of support, help and understanding.

In a break with tradition I have used the Western dating system throughout so that readers can parallel events elsewhere in the world without the tedium of adding 13 to Russian dates until February 1918.

Introduction

The First World War was the catalyst for a wide variety of political and sociological changes across the face of the globe; of these one of the most important for the history of the twentieth century and beyond were the Russian revolutions of 1917. The roots of these events lay in the decade before 1914 so an understanding of this period of Russian history is essential, as is the fact that the Russian empire was exactly that – a land-based empire made up of diverse races, religious persuasions, languages, cultures and aspirations held in place by the increasingly moribund power of one family, the house of Romanov.

Until 1905 the Tsar of Russia held almost absolute power over the 150 million people of his domains. This system of government worked well enough until two factors came into play. The first of these was military defeat that undermined faith in the Tsar's judgement and infallibility. The second was the perception of his personal weakness of character exemplified by indecisiveness. Both strands came together during and immediately following the defeat of Russia by Japan in 1905. The failure of Russia's armed forces coincided with civil unrest which, at first confined to the major cities, rapidly spread across the empire and led to a spate of peasant uprisings. The Tsar, under pressure from his advisors, granted a constitution based on a relatively liberal franchise. However, as the disturbances died down the Tsar regained confidence in his former autocratic powers, and consequently he modified the franchise and curbed the powers of the Duma, the newly created parliament. As a result, the political condition of Russia was unsteady until economic and industrial expansion, combined with land reform, reduced overt discontent with the regime.

With the establishment of the Duma, even with a limited franchise and negligible legislative and executive powers, the political parties from left to right at least had a legal forum in which to express their opinions. The more outspoken politicians, for example Vladimir Lenin, were in exile in Western Europe or in the case of those found guilty of criminal activities including bank robbery or murder, such as Stalin, imprisoned or exiled within Russia itself.

Relative financial stability was accompanied by rapid industrial expansion which was based on overseas investment and the exploitation of Russia's vast, untapped natural resources. Part of the increased tax revenue that resulted was spent on improving the strength of the armed forces, which grew rapidly in size and modernity.

By 1914 such was the internal condition of Russia that it seemed unlikely that it would ever experience a revolution. Indeed, when war broke out during the first week of August 1914 the only members of the Duma who voted against war credits were the two Bolshevik representatives.

The command of Russia's armed forces was placed in the hands of the Grand Duke Nicholas, the Tsar's first cousin. The Grand Duke had the misfortune to preside over a calamitous 12 months for the empire's military. The invasions of East Prussia and eastern Germany were rebuffed, although the Austro-Hungarian forces were driven back to the Carpathian Mountains. The early months of 1915 were marked by a munitions shortage which reduced the army's capacity to resist a powerful Austro-German offensive that drove Russia from its Polish territories and much occupied Austro-Hungarian land.

When the line stabilized in the late summer of 1915 the Russian armies were reorganized into three army groups known as Fronts. The Northern Front ran from the Baltic Sea to its junction with the Western Front near Lake Narotch and then the South-Western Front took over from south of the Pripet Marshes down to the Romanian border. When the Grand Duke Nicholas was replaced by the Tsar he went to command the Caucasian Front, successfully fighting the Ottoman Turks in eastern Anatolia.

Although the Russian Army had performed poorly during the first year of the war, reforms were in train which by mid-1916 had borne fruit. The achievement of the South-Western Front's summer offensive, the so-called Brusilov Offensive, signified the high-water mark of the war on the Eastern Front. Unfortunately, defeating the Austro-Hungarian Army did not bring more than temporary relief and during the autumn of that year morale in the army and on the home front declined dramatically. Talk amongst the politicians in Petrograd revolved around a change in the empire's government.

The sparks that ignited the March Revolution were a combination of food shortages, labour unrest and disloyalty – amongst the military the Petrograd garrison sided with the demonstrators. When the Tsar attempted to return to his capital to restore order he was delayed by railway workers and thus whilst in limbo was advised to abdicate by his Front commanders, which he did on 15 March 1917.

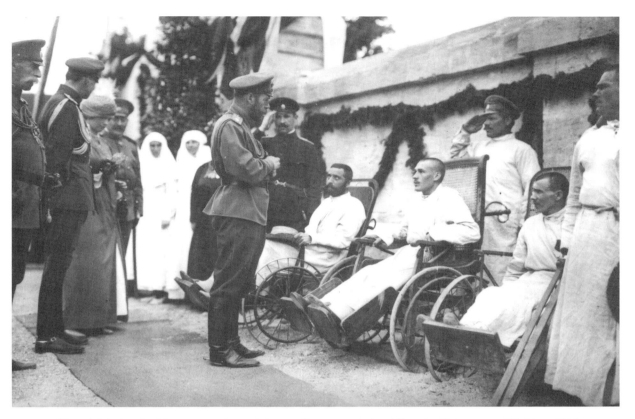

Tsar Nicholas II visits a convalescent home for wounded soldiers in Odessa on 23 May 1916. Nicholas' tenure as Supreme Commander in Chief of the Russian Armed Forces began during the summer of 1915 and lasted until his abdication on 15 March 1917. He was an indifferent soldier and figurehead who commanded little respect other than that conferred by his position.

Whilst the Tsar vegetated at Stavka (army headquarters), his wife, the Tsaritsa Alexandra, remained in Petrograd. Seen here with her son the Tsarevitch Alexis on the back steps of the Winter Palace, Alexandra exercised an allegedly malign influence over her husband. The rumours of her pro-German sentiments played no little part in undermining the position and authority of the autocracy.

Although not as widespread as later accounts implied, there were instances of Russian troops disobeying orders and refusing to fight. Nevertheless, at the inter-Allied conference held in Petrograd in January 1917, the Russians promised a mighty summer offensive that was conditional upon receiving substantial quantities of munitions from France and Britain.

Refugees from the western provinces of Russia prepare to bed down for the night. This vast movement of people, numbering over 2 million, combined with the poorly administered railway system, grain hoarding in the provinces and a shortage of basic foodstuffs, led to growing social unrest particularly in the capital Petrograd.

A sense of calm spread across the entire front from the Baltic to the Black seas and Russian troops began to fraternize with their erstwhile enemies. Here men of the Russian and Austro-Hungarian armies pose for the camera in April 1917. As their authority diminished, Russian officers were unable and often unwilling to prevent such fraternal events.

A Cossack regiment, part of the Northern Front, prepares to swear allegiance to the Provisional Government in late March 1917. At such ceremonies Tsarist symbols were usually discarded or covered in red ribbons.

Chapter One

Events in Petrograd are Far from Calm

Nicholas' abdication was met with almost universal jubilation, tinged with not a little relief that virtually no one had raised a hand in protest. Having, illegally under Russia's Fundamental Law, abdicated for his sickly son and himself, the former Tsar had granted succession to his brother, the Grand Duke Michael. The Grand Duke declared that he would only accept the title should it be granted to him, 'by our great people … through its representatives in the Constituent Assembly'.

The Constituent Assembly was to be Russia's new parliament, elected by universal suffrage in the near future. During the time lapse between the end of the monarchy and the establishment of the Constituent Assembly a collection of committees and ministers entitled the Provisional Government would lead Russia. The Provisional Government was cobbled together on 15 March from members of the last Duma. Simultaneously, a more radical group had formed the Petrograd Soviet of Workers and Soldier's Deputies ('soviet' being the Russian word for council). From the outset both groups monitored each other's activities and utterances with deep suspicion. Politically, the members of the Provisional Government tended to be democratically liberal with few socialist policies; in the main it was made up of members of the Cadet (Constitutional Democratic) Party. The Soviet, on the other hand, had assembled on 12 March and formed an Executive Committee which limited membership to representatives of specific socialist parties. Therefore, although the Provisional Government was the apparently legal authority, the Soviet exerted a significant influence from the outset. Symptomatic of this power was the issuing of the infamous Order Number 1 which granted soldiers and sailors a variety of rights, such as the election of unit committees (down to company level) to control arms, armoured cars, artillery, machine guns and side arms and to elect representatives who would speak for them in the Petrograd Soviet. Order Number 1 also conferred the right to disobey orders that were at odds with those issued by the Petrograd Soviet. However,

Order Number 1 was intended to apply only to the Petrograd garrison with the purpose of stifling any counter-revolutionary activity by officers. But, knowledge of its contents soon spread through the rear areas and reached the front lines. Within days the officer corps was marginalized as soldiers and sailors embraced their new found freedom with delight, gathering to hold meetings at the slightest opportunity. So widespread was this phenomenon that a verb was coined to describe it – *mitingovat*, to 'meetingify'.

Considering how momentous the events of early March were, there was remarkably little violence and few casualties. Almost no one raised a hand in defence of the dynasty or the old order. There were two senior cavalry officers that offered their units to restore the monarchy but they were ignored, and the former Tsar joined his wife and children in protective custody at Tsarskoe Selo. By a twist of fate the Tsaritsa had been informed of her arrest by the new commander of the Petrograd Military District, General of Infantry L. G. Kornilov, of whom much more would be heard during the following 12 months. For the army the revolution was remarkably bloodless but for the navy, particularly the Baltic Sea Fleet at its main base on the fortress island of Kronstadt near Petrograd, it was a different matter. Scores of officers, including the fleet's commander, had been murdered. However, as dozens of cities, towns and provinces across Russia elected soviets of varying shades of leftist political opinions, the nation's future hung in the balance whilst the Provisional Government considered the future and how to balance the demands of so many interest groups against a background of debate, confusion and above all an ongoing world war.

The Petrograd Soviet and the general public were ambivalent towards the prosecution of the war, whereas the Provisional Government was in favour of honouring the former regime's obligations to carry on fighting. When, in early May, the Foreign Minister P. N. Miliukov declared that Russia would adhere to the Imperial government's treaty obligations regarding the war and the rewards Russia would expect, which included former enemy territory, there was an outcry from the socialist parties. The so-called April Crisis (under the old dating system) resulted in the resignation of Miliukov and the War Minster A. I. Guchkov. A. F. Kerensky, supported by the Soviet, took Guchkov's place. There was now a new coalition Provisional Government that included representatives of the Social Revolutionary (SR) and Menshevik parties. The SRs were the major force in the Petrograd Soviet, however; their position was under threat from the Bolsheviks whose leader V. I. Lenin had returned from exile in Switzerland with German cooperation.

Lenin was ruthless, adaptable and calculating but above all focused on one thing – the achievement of power for the Bolsheviks. To do this he insisted on party discipline and was consequently intolerant of internal dissent. From the outset he made his party's programme clear. Avoiding wordy phraseology, his pithy declarations of 'All Power to the Soviet and peace, bread and land' struck a chord with the vast mass of his listeners. Nevertheless, he recognized the need to move cautiously and garner support. Power was Lenin's goal and he was not prepared to jeopardize his opportunity by premature action from a position of political or military weakness. The first objective Lenin targeted was an increase in Bolshevik representation on the Petrograd Soviet. Meanwhile, Kerensky was not idle. Having secured support for the war from the soviet, he undertook a tour of the front lines to address staffs, officers and the rank and file to enthuse them with his own brand of motivational speaking. A born performer and orator, Kerensky achieved a veneer of success and returned to Petrograd convinced that the upcoming summer offensive, conducted by the 'freest army in the world', would sweep all before it. The Russian high command, Stavka, the Front commanders and the Supreme Commander in Chief General M. V. Alexeyev were less sanguine. Alexeyev was replaced, along with hundreds of other senior officers, by General A. A. Brusilov who was a more bellicose leader and an adherent of Kerensky's policies, as well as a renowned strategist. Unfortunately, when the offensive began on 1 July 1917, although it made some headway, the enthusiasm instilled by Kerensky's speeches proved hollow as many of the supporting troops refused to back the advance. The situation quickly deteriorated and within days troops of the South-Western Front, the main attacking force (Kornilov's new command), were in retreat, fleeing in many cases before inferior opposition as far back as the Russian border. By re-imposing the death penalty in the field and organizing punitive formations from the more loyal elements of his army group, Kornilov re-established the front. However, in Petrograd the Bolsheviks took advantage of the situation at the front to attempt a coup. For several days in mid-July the position of the Provisional Government looked decidedly uncertain as troops and sailors from Kronstadt paraded through Petrograd in an attempt to take power. Lenin wanted no truck with what he viewed as a foolish undertaking but was swept along by events. By 18 July the arrival of men loyal to the Provisional Government and the skilful use of propaganda that purported to prove that the Bolshevik leadership was in the pay of the Germans scuttled the 'uprising'. Kerensky now assumed the mantle of Minister President as well as Minister of War and promptly installed Kornilov as Supreme Commander in Chief of the Armed Forces. Kornilov's appointment was applauded by those on the right who felt that the revolution had moved too far to the left. They saw in him a personality who would save Russia from anarchy, as it was put – a man on a white horse – even a potential military dictator. To cap everything, on 25 July Finland demanded independence, with Ukraine calling for similar autonomy in certain affairs including the establishment of a separate army.

At the front the army regained its composure as Kornilov pressed for the reintroduction of discipline and the affirmation of the death penalty for the armed forces. Indeed, officers regained their confidence to issue orders the rank and file usually obeyed, although sometimes resentfully. As the summer drew on a meeting was called to be known as the Moscow State Conference with the declared intention of 'restoring national unity'. It was timed for the last week of August. Only the Bolshevik Party declined to attend. Kornilov and Kerensky were both present, the latter receiving a warm welcome from the right wing which irritated Kerensky not a little.

When the Germans launched a surprise attack and Riga fell on 3 September Kornilov placed the blame on cowardice and Bolshevized mutineers. However, this time Kornilov's criticisms were not championed by Kerensky. Supporters of both rallied behind their leaders. There then followed a strange incident known as the Kornilov Affair. Kornilov was assembling a force, the Petrograd Army, to defend the capital against the anticipated German advance along the coastline. It was to consist of troops who were felt to be resistant to the negative influence of the Petrograd Soviet, such as the Caucasian Native Cavalry Corps, a unit comprising Moslem Caucasian tribesmen and other mounted formations, such as III Cavalry Corps, who had resisted the worst excesses of the committees system and the decay of discipline since the revolution. Kornilov, who was described by his predecessor Brusilov as having 'the courage of a lion but the brains of a goat', appeared to be bidding to topple the Provisional Government and the Petrograd Soviet. Kerensky therefore issued orders to arm the city's workers (thus resurrecting the Red Guards banned since the July Days), and dispatched agitators to convince the Caucasians of Kornilov's duplicity – he had claimed that they were going to Petrograd to suppress a counter-revolution. The agitators achieved their purpose and other troops were held up by railway workers. Thus Kornilov's attempt to seize power failed.

Kornilov was arrested along with several of his supporters and imprisoned in a monastery, Bykhovo prison, near Stavka at Mogilev to await trial. But now Kerensky found himself increasingly isolated and threatened by the Petrograd Soviet. The capital itself was apparently at the mercy of the Germans as by late October they had overrun the islands off the coast of Latvia and Estonia. By this time the Bolsheviks were in control of the Petrograd Soviet under the chairmanship of L. D. Trotsky, Lenin's more aggressive subordinate, who formed the Military Revolutionary Committee (RMC) which effectively took control of the Petrograd Military District on 4 November.

Neatly timed to implicate the national congress of delegates from soviets all over Russia, the Bolsheviks struck on 7 November. The cabinet of the Provisional Government was arrested in the Winter Palace and strategic locations such as the telegraph office were also occupied. Lenin's Bolsheviks had taken control of the capital in the name of the soviets but they had not captured Kerensky. In an effort to raise support Kerensky had fled to Pskov, the HQ of the Northern Front, from where he called for loyal troops. The only support he gathered was the III Cavalry Corps commanded by General P. N. Krasnov, a Don Cossack, as were most of his troops, although only roughly 1,000 rallied behind him. Stalemated at Pulkovo Heights, Kerensky's support withered and he eventually left Russia. As the news of the Bolshevik triumph spread across Russia some men's thoughts turned to what to do about it.

Marines of the Guard march to the Tauride Palace, headquarters of the Provisional Government, to swear allegiance to the new administration. Commanded by the Grand Duke Kirill Romanov, cousin and brother-in-law of the former Tsar, this display of support for the new regime left many in no doubt that few if any were prepared to fight for Nicholas.

Early in the reign of the Provisional Government nationalist sentiment came to the fore. Within days of the revolution, both Poland and Finland were promised changes in their circumstances following the end of the war. Here Estonian troops in the Russian Army parade through Petrograd. The banner proclaims, 'Long live the Russian Federative Republic and autonomous Estonia'. Ukraine and the Caucasian provinces would shortly demand similar privileges.

By late March the Western powers and the USA had recognized the Provisional Government as the legitimate authority in Russia. However, various socialist representatives of those governments visited the Petrograd Soviet providing it with a veneer of international recognition as a source of power. Here two British Labour Party MPs, Will Thorne and James O'Grady (centre wearing homburgs), mingle with Soviet delegates.

Sergeant Timofei Kirpichnikov, who led the mutiny of the Volynsky Guard Regiment that brought the Petrograd garrison over to the side of the revolutionaries. The St George's cross he is wearing was awarded by the Petrograd Soviet on 19 April for his bravery and leadership.

A group of Kuban Cossack officers poses for the camera behind the front line. Even the Cossacks were beginning to consider breaking away from Russian rule. No longer were they prepared to be the unthinking policemen of any regime. In specialist formations, such as the Cossacks and the artillery, officers still retained their previous authority.

At the front the Central Powers adopted a wait and see approach to events. There was only one battle of significance on the Stokhod River during the first week of April. German troops eliminated a Russian bridgehead on the western bank, taking 10,000 POWs in the process. The Moscow Soviet blamed traitors in high places, others indiscipline and staff incompetence. The real villains were surprise and gas.

The two-brigade Russian Expeditionary Force in France had arrived on the Western Front in 1916. In May 1917 the 1st Brigade mutinied. Its 1st regiment was composed of urban workers who adopted a more militant attitude. The regiment was isolated and contained until the autumn as the French had to cope with mutinies in their own army. The other brigade remained loyal to the Provisional Government. This state of affairs was representative of events in the East, the units from the towns being initially more heavily politicized than those from the countryside.

A major cause of pre-revolution grievance was the conscription of family men over 40. In April all men over 43 and those over 40 in rear units were discharged from the service. They were unofficially joined by many from the front line who felt it was their right to go home. The result was thousands of ex-soldiers congregating in the cities; they had nothing to do and acted as a focus for agitators.

In an attempt to shame their men into a more active, martial mentality several volunteer battalions of women were formed. In the main a propaganda exercise that failed, only one unit was sent to the front where it went into action and suffered heavy losses.

A more effective measure was the formation of Shock or Death Battalions from front-line and rear-area units. Identified by badges and chevrons, these volunteers acquitted themselves with distinction during the July Offensive. The badge seen here is that of the best known shock formation, the Kornilov Regiment.

Members of the Royal Naval Armoured Car Division, Britain's contribution to the Russian Front, in the trenches. Placed with the attacking forces to encourage the Russians by their example, the British later found themselves used to cover the Russian retreat. They returned to Britain in late 1917.

With the failure of the Summer Offensive the front once more settled down with the exception of the Romanian Front. However, the summer was marked by recriminations in Petrograd as to why the offensive had failed. As accusations flew in all directions the Bolsheviks increased their propaganda activities amongst the troops.

Kornilov's replacement as commander of the Petrograd Military District, General P. A. Polovtsov (centre in light uniform), was more politically astute than his predecessor. Polovtsov's tact and approach to command were significant in keeping the troops under control during the July Days.

Kerensky, pictured here observing the first day of the summer offensive, 1 July 1917, was a brilliant orator and a man of high principle dedicated to a bloodless, honourable revolution. He did not execute Trotsky following the July Days, nor Kornilov following the abortive putsch in August. A solicitor by profession, he was determined to 'play fair' which cost him his ambitions for a democratic Russia and almost his life.

The outside of the Bolshevik Party's HQ, Kshesinsky Palace. The failure of the attempted *coup d'état* resulted in Lenin's flight to Finland and Trotsky's imprisonment. There was much subsequent disagreement in Bolshevik ranks about the restraint ordered by their leaders.

Throughout the summer of 1917 the Bolsheviks set about increasing their propaganda and recruitment activities amongst the front-line troops. Here Bolshevik agitators, in civilian dress, pose with some of their audience in the trenches. Other parties, notably the SR, conducted similar tours.

Some of the Provisional Government's defenders at the Winter Palace were members of the Women's Battalion of Death. Contrary to legend, the last bastion of the Provisional Government was occupied not stormed and the women and officer cadets were sent home by the Bolsheviks. There was more fighting in Moscow, but again casualties were light.

Triumphant Bolshevik soldiers and Red Guards brew up outside the Admiralty building on Palace Square.

Kornilov (centre in white fur cap) surrounded by Cossack troops.

After their victory at Pulkovo Heights, Red Guards and soldiers pose for the camera. Krasnov and the Cossacks were allowed to return to their homes in the Don region having given their word not to take up arms again. The first shots of the Russian Civil War had been fired, the next would not be long in coming.

Chapter Two

A Time of Confusion and Hope

By way of contrast to the March revolution that of November 1917 involved fighting from the outset. The defeat of Kerensky's scratch force of Cossacks at the battle of Pulkovo Heights was, however, followed by a period of intense negotiation between the Bolsheviks and the Social Revolutionary Party (SR). The SRs resented the unilateral manner in which the Bolsheviks had taken power. However, the SRs lacked military muscle and were themselves far from a united body so there was little they could do. Indeed, a significant minority of the more radical SRs aligned themselves with the Bolsheviks during December. With the coalition of the Left SRs, as they became known, and the Bolsheviks the SR Party itself accepted the situation and sat back to await the results of the elections to the Constituent Assembly that had just been held, confident of gaining a working majority. Voting for the Constituent Assembly was remarkably democratic; the franchise included men and women over 20 with no property qualification and members of the armed forces without exception. The SRs gained 50 per cent of the vote, the Bolsheviks 24 per cent. Including nationalist groups in Ukraine, the Caucasus and elsewhere, less than 20 per cent of the votes went to non-socialist parties. The Cadets polled less than 5 per cent and were outlawed as counter-revolutionary by the Bolsheviks immediately after the election. This led to an exodus of Cadet politicians and their more prominent supporters from Petrograd and Moscow to the Don Cossack region and points east. Other political groups of centrist or right-wing persuasion followed or adopted a lower profile.

Political power in the major cities and regional centres rested with the local soviets. The membership of the soviets witnessed a steady polarization as the Bolsheviks and Left SRs jockeyed for control with the SRs. Support for the SRs was based on the peasantry, whereas the Bolsheviks and Left SRs relied on the armed forces and industrial centres for the majority of their backing. Indeed, the Bolsheviks had achieved well over 50 per cent of the soldiers' votes, this rising to 67 per cent in the Baltic Sea Fleet.

Having gained control of Petrograd, and with the first sitting of the Constituent Assembly timed for the early weeks of 1918, Lenin knew he had to move fast to present the nation with peace prior to worldwide revolution. Consequently, the armed forces had to be brought under legal control. To expedite this he dispatched Lieutenant N. V. Krylenko to Stavka at Mogilev to replace the Supreme Commander in Chief General N. N. Dukhonin.

Although Dukhonin had called for troops loyal to the Provisional Government to protect Stavka, they did not arrive in time having failed to fight their way through pro-Bolshevik formations. Dukhonin was murdered as rumours spread about the escape of Kornilov and his co-conspirators from their gaol nearby. As Krylenko stepped over the corpse of his predecessor negotiations began with the Central Powers for an armistice. This began on 15 December. It was, of course, a disaster for the Allies who now cast about for Russians prepared to continue the war and they settled on Kaledin's Don Cossacks.

To Westerners the Cossacks represented martial vigour, honour and simple loyalty. That this was a misconception was nonetheless ignored and plans were laid to provide Kaledin with millions of pounds to fund an army to fight against the Central Powers and restore the Eastern Front. However, in Novocherkassk, the capital of the Don Cossack region, a new force was gathering – the Volunteer Army. A former Supreme Commander in Chief, General M. V. Alexeyev, had made his way to the Don Cossacks at the invitation of their Ataman (leader) General A. M. Kaledin. Kaledin had been sympathetic to Kornilov's attempted coup and had been trying to rally the support of other Cossack *Hosts* (nations), such as those of the Kuban and the Terek, to organize a Cossack regional government in opposition to the Bolsheviks. This Cossack federation failed to materialize but Alexeyev began to recruit for his Volunteer Army (VA). Unfortunately for both Kaledin and Alexeyev, the younger Cossack veterans were unsympathetic to their cause and the few recruits the VA attracted were former officers and military cadets.

On 19 December Kornilov himself arrived in Novocherkassk. Now, alongside generals A. I. Denikin and I. P. Romanovsky the command structure of the VA was established. Alexeyev took charge of domestic and foreign affairs and Kornilov military affairs and command of the army. Politically they were advised by senior Cadet Party members and moderate socialists. The VA declared its aims to be, 'the restoration of a Free, Great Russia . . .' and to 'stand guard over civil liberties [until] the Russian people can express its will through the election of a Constituent Assembly'. But even these apparently fine ideals did not encourage an influx of recruits.

Early in 1918 the Bolsheviks were gathering their forces to eliminate Kaledin and the embryonic VA. As they assembled Kaledin was informed that the VA was leaving the Don region for the apparently safer haven of the Kuban region.

Numbering 3,500 men and hauling a few pieces of artillery, the VA embarked upon what became known as the Ice March. In its wake trailed a motley collection of politicians and other civilians for whom the Don lands had become too hot for them to stay in. The Ice March lasted for 80 days and during that time the VA trekked over 1,100km fighting on 44 days as it sought to avoid destruction and raise support amongst the Kuban Cossack Host.

Meanwhile, in Petrograd the elected representatives from across Russia began to arrive to take their seats in the Constituent Assembly. They fondly believed that long-deferred decisions on the future of Russia's new regime would now be taken and that the country would enter into a bold, new and prosperous future. But few of those crossing the snowy wastes had calculated on the ruthlessness of Lenin. Dragging his often argumentative and disaffected supporters along with him, Lenin had encouraged the growth of an anti-Constituent Assembly bloc. When the Constituent Assembly finally opened on 18 January it descended into farce. In a hall packed with an audience of drunken revellers who jeered and catcalled at any and every opportunity the sitting nearly broke up. The following day armed Bolshevik supporters forced the members to dissolve the assembly. Faced with naked force they left for their homes. Now, with the Constituent Assembly eliminated, the army demobilizing and units of Red Guards and Bolshevik sailors scouring the countryside for food to avoid a repeat of the previous year's supply problems, Lenin's position looked relatively secure.

But, as Trotsky discussed the peace terms in Brest Litovsk, there were those in Russia who were horrified at the manner of the dissolution of the Constituent Assembly and the cavalier attitude of the Bolsheviks and the Left SRs. In Ukraine there was fighting between Red Guards and the forces of the Ukrainian nationalists under S.V. Petlyura. Delegates from Ukraine had appeared at Brest Litovsk determined to sign a separate peace with the Central Powers and thus gain recognition for their regime, known as the Rada. This they achieved but Russia was not prepared to give way as easily. Trotsky was ordered to prevaricate as Lenin was convinced that central Europe would swiftly follow Russia into revolution. Trotsky left Brest Litovsk declaring that the final phase of Russian demobilization would begin and that a period of 'no peace and no war' now existed. This galvanized the Central Powers into action and with the end of the armistice on 18 February Austro-German forces once again attacked.

Acutely aware that Russia was incapable of defending itself, Lenin sued for peace but now it was the turn of the Central Powers to sidestep the question. On 23 February Germany issued fresh terms that included the loss to Russia of Finland, the Baltic provinces of Lithuania, Latvia and Estonia as well as Ukraine and a zone of occupation that stretched as far as Rostov on Don in the south, Kursk in the centre and the borders of Estonia in the north. Horrified at the loss of vast swathes of farming land, mineral resources and population, many of Lenin's supporters as well as those of other political parties, particularly the SRs, called for a resumption of hostilities. Lenin refused and on 3 March 1918 the revised Treaty of Brest Litovsk was signed by a mainly Bolshevik delegation. Consequently, the Left SRs promptly abandoned their coalition with the Bolsheviks. Now alone, Lenin's party still controlled the majority of the soviets across Russia and by dint of the Red Guards effectively dominated the political arena. It was at this point that the array of other political groups should have united in opposition to the Bolsheviks but such was their mutual antagonism that such a coalition did not develop. The seeds were sown for a four-way split in Russia, best described as the Red, White, Green and Black 'Guards'. Red for the Bolsheviks, white for those based around the former army, green for the SRs and their adherents and black for the anarchists. Generally, the nationalists were lumped in together with the White Guards by the Bolshevik propaganda machine to which all non-Bolsheviks were counter-revolutionaries. Not all these groups used these colourful terms to describe themselves but the labels are helpful particularly since the Bolsheviks called for volunteers to join the Worker's and Peasant's Red Army on 23 February 1918.

Far away on the Kuban steppe the VA was at its last gasp. Having failed to take Ekaterinodar, capital of the Kuban region, and having lost Kornilov to a stray shell, it headed north. However, good news awaited Denikin, the new military commander of the VA, and Alexeyev that the Don Cossacks had risen against the Bolshevik regime in their region, and were forming an army to liberate the region led by General P. N. Krasnov, last heard of at Pulkovo Heights commanding Kerensky's forlorn hope. By mid-April the Don Cossacks had expelled the Red Guards from the Don lands.

But in Ukraine the Germans had on 29 April replaced Petlyura's regime with a puppet government of their own led by Hetman (leader) General P. P. Skoropadsky. Now the Austro-German forces of occupation could begin to exploit the food resources of Ukraine. For the Western allies reeling under the hammer blows of Germany's latest offensive it was vital that Russia, whatever its regime, be encouraged to return to the fight.

Private Pavel Zherdev poses in an early war photograph. Zherdev was a supporter of the Bolshevik revolution and went on to serve in the Red Army during the civil war. He rose to the rank of First Commissar for a region on the Volga River but was executed during the Stalinist purges of the 1930s.

Dispatch riders at Stavka. By the autumn of 1917 Allied representatives, diplomatic and military, had converged on the Stavka to encourage Russia to keep fighting. The last thing they wished to see was Russia leaving the war thus releasing German and Austrian troops to operate on other fronts.

A group of Austro-Hungarian armistice negotiators waits for talks to begin. It was vital for the Central Powers, particularly Austria-Hungary, to achieve a settlement as food stuffs were in short supply and civil unrest threatened. When the armistice was concluded it rolled on in 30-day periods.

Officer cadets such as this man provided a large percentage of the Volunteer Army in its early days. Few were monarchists and such recruits were mainly concerned with preserving the achievements of the Provisional Government and Russia's honour by reforming the front against the Central Powers.

A Don Cossack, proudly displaying his St George's cross won fighting the Germans, of the type Alexeyev and the Allies hoped to rally to the cause of continuing the war. When the brutal realities of Bolshevik rule became apparent, thousands of men such as this flocked to join the Don Army to fight for a free homeland.

27 февраля 1917 года

КРАСНАЯ ГВАРДІЯ

Васильевского Острова

Formed on an ad hoc basis across Russia following the March Revolution to protect the Soviets, the Red Guards became progressively more organized as 1917 drew on. By early 1918 they numbered over 200,000, their ranks swelled by demobilized soldiers. The arm band is that of the Red Guard detachment, on Vassilievsky Island, Petrograd. Many Red Guardsmen went into the ranks of the Red Army.

Kornilov (seen here on the left in Austrian captivity in 1915) arrived in Novocherkassk at the same time as the force that was to form the nucleus of the VA, the Kornilov Shock Regiment raised in June 1917 and named in his honour.

A poster calling for recruits to the Red Army as issued in Moscow city and district. By the end of April some 200,000 had volunteered. At first a lack of numbers in the volunteer force numbers led to the imposition of conscription from May 1918 for all men aged between 18 and 40.

Товарищи рабочіе, солдаты и крестьяне, организуйте свои силы, стройте свою красную армію!

Для нашей революціи настал грозный и рѣшительный час. Помѣщики и капиталисты не могут примириться с политикой Совѣтской Власти. Мы сломили сопротивленіе их внутри Россіи. На их помощь, испугавшись нашей революціи, спѣшит буржуазія других стран. Она идет против нашей республики своих юнкеров и бѣлогвардейцев.

Крестьяне! Совѣтская власть отняла у помѣщиков землю и отдала ее вам.

Рабочіе! Совѣтская власть освободила вас от гнета капиталистов и поставила под ваш контроль заводы и фабрики.

Солдаты! Совѣтская власть добивалась всеобщаго демократическаго мира, нужно было вывести измученныя армiи из залитых кровью траншей. Совѣтская делегація в Брестѣ громко сказала международному пролетаріату: Довольно крови! Твоя очередь! Разбей власть капитала! Она объявила войну на наших фронтах оконченной. Совѣтская власть кончила войну нашего народа с другими народами.

Но сильна еще власть международнаго капитала. Буржуазія двинула своих юнкеров и бѣлогвардейцев против нашей республики.

Из Румынiи идут ударные батальоны на помощь бессарабским помѣщикам. Они громят Совѣты, возвращают земли помѣщикам, водворяют старые порядки.

Германское правительство осадным положеніем задавило на время рабочее движеніе, бросило свою бѣлую гвардію на наши деревни и города. К ней присоединились легіоны польской шляхты. Под ея покровительством стала украинская рада, поставив свои вооруженныя силы рядом с германскими батальонами.

Эти силы быстро двигаются вперед, онѣ спѣшат,—пока еще не разразилась революція в Германіи, пока на мѣсто демобилизованной армiи мы не развернули батальоны новой красной армiи.

Они спѣшат уничтожить всѣ наши завоеванія, они надѣются на новое возстаніе контр-революціонных сил внутри Россіи. И контр-революція притаилась, ждет удобнаго момента.

Товарищи! Грозный час настал. Каждый час дорог. Стройте свои батальоны, записывайтесь в ряды красной армiи. К оружію, товарищи!

Успѣем ли мы? Подойдем ли во время? Быть может, Совѣтская власть добьется новаго перемирія. Каждый час его мы используем для организаціи нашей боевой силы.

Близок час международной революціи.

Да здравствует красная революціонная армія! К оружію, товарищи!

Да здравствует власть совѣтов!

Да здравствует 3-й интернаціонал!

Президіумъ С. Р., С. и кр. Депутатов гор. Москвы и Московской области.

Men of the Russian Caucasian Army in the process of withdrawing from the Turkish Front pause to eat. The Turks, following slowly in their wake, were bent on re-establishing control over the Caucasus.

Under the supplementary terms of the Treaty of Brest-Litovsk (dated August 1918) Georgia became an independent state. The price was 25 per cent of Georgia's oil production. These Georgian officers are gathered to celebrate the establishment of the Trans-Caucasion Federation in May 1918 which paved the way for Georgian independence.

A Russian picket, armed with a British-made Lewis gun, defends what was left of the front following the demobilization of the army on 10 February 1918. Groups like this could do nothing to halt Operation Thunderbolt, the German advance into Russia, which began the same month.

Field Marshal von Eichorn, commander of the Austro-German occupation forces in Ukraine, inspects Ukrainian troops in Kiev. Ukraine was the breadbasket of Russia and although the Bolshevik troops were driven out, they continued to agitate against the occupation amongst the peasantry.

Fighting alongside the Bolsheviks in Ukraine were elements of the Czech Legion. Formed in 1914 and expanded to corps size by early 1918, the Legion, recruited from Czech POWs and deserters from the Austro-Hungarian Army, was a force to be reckoned with. Driven from its base in Ukraine, the 40,000-strong Czech Legion moved eastwards, planning to evacuate to Europe via Vladivostock.

To reach Vladivostock it would be necessary for the Czech Legion to use the Trans-Siberian railway. As the lead units began the journey encounters with returning Austro-Hungarian and German troops became increasingly fraught, as did relations with the Bolsheviks. Following an incident on 14 May 1918 the Czechs decided that they had no option but to fight their way across Siberia. With their echelons spread along the 9,600km-length of the railway they became its effective masters.

The Austro-German occupation of Ukraine was simply an exercise in pillage. To relieve food shortages in Germany, and in particular Austria, requisitioning parties scoured the countryside for supplies. Anyone resisting was dealt with summarily, as seen here. Retaliation and self-defence led to increasing levels of violence by nationalist and other political groups.

If any of the early Red Army's formations could be designated elite then it was the Latvian Rifle regiments. Raised during the First World War, many of the riflemen were convinced Bolsheviks. They fought on almost every front during the civil war. This image here dates from pre-Soviet times.

To bring a degree of technical expertise to the Red Army Trotsky enrolled thousands of former Tsarist officers. Known as *Voyenspets*, military specialists, the lives of their families often depended on their loyalty to their new employers. Groups, such as those seen here, or individuals often deserted at the first opportunity. Others, such as General A. A. Brusilov, gave loyal service.

Another ubiquitous force during the civil war was the sailors, mainly from the Baltic Fleet who were staunch supporters of the Bolshevik regime. Generally retaining their naval uniform, they were feared by all their opponents. This seaman is from the *Diana*, sister ship to the *Aurora* which fired on the Winter Palace in support of the Bolshevik coup in 1917.

Slowly at first but with increasing momentum as the year drew on, thousands of Austro-German POWs began the long journey home from Siberia and Central Asia. Some amongst them joined the Red Army to stay and fight for 'World Revolution'. The POWs were a source of great concern for the Allies who believed them to be a potential advanced guard for the German domination of Siberia and beyond.

One of the major weapons of the civil war was the armoured train. They were built, extemporized or captured and used by all sides. With the absence of a continuous front line the forward position of such a monolith often marked the front line. The train seen here is part of a Red Army unit.

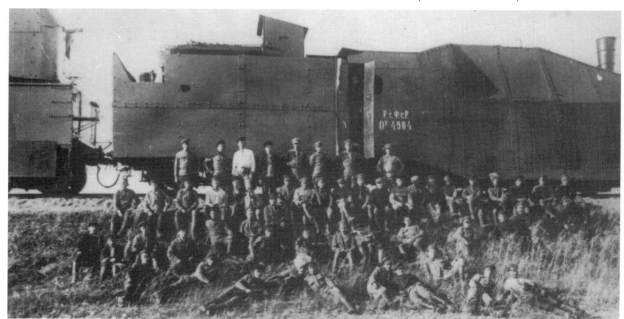

Chapter Three

The Opposition Emerges

By 5 March 1918 the fear of Germany overrunning Petrograd had prompted Lenin to move his seat of government to Moscow. However, the Allied diplomatic corps had transferred itself to Vologda, well sited to reach both Petrograd and Moscow by rail as well as Archangel should evacuation prove necessary. When the German offensive began on the Western Front on 21 March its success was such that reviving the Russian Front became, in the minds of Western politicians, essential. The British believed that some form of deal involving Allied support could be done with Trotsky. One such idea envisaged sending Japanese soldiers along the Trans-Siberian railway to fight the Central Powers in European Russia. However, once again, Trotsky prevaricated to gain time. In the words of Lord Milner, Secretary of State for War, 'it is desirable to work as well as we can with the Bolshevik Government'. Practically speaking, the most conveniently situated Allied force was the Czech Legion, with the bulk of its 45,000 men still west of the Ural Mountains. The British proposed sending 20,000 Czechs to the northern ports of Murmansk and Archangel to protect thousands of tons of imported munitions, bought by the Tsarist and Provisional governments that were awaiting shipment south, from the anticipated German advance into Finland. Allied command in this region that would include the Czechs would be in the hands of British General F. C. Poole. As the Austro-German armies advanced across Ukraine the fate of the Russian Black Sea Fleet in Sevastopol became an increasing concern. What would the Bolsheviks order its sailors to do when the Germans arrived? Scuttle, fight or steam off to another port to the east? Of equal concern was the Baltic Sea Fleet, much of which was located in Finnish waters and thus in danger from the Germans who were expected to arrive daily.

Far away on the Pacific coast the Bolsheviks were in control of Vladivostok and furiously shipping supplies from the vast munitions dumps there to the west, but such were local conditions that the Allied representatives there were unsure what the final destination of these weapons would be. When Japanese marines were landed in Vladivostok on 4 April 'to protect their empire's interests in the city' Trotsky's attitude to Allied assistance became less welcoming.

The British War Cabinet's confusion, paralleled by that of its men on the ground all over Russia, was a major feature of this period. The Bolsheviks did not trust the Allies, particularly since the repudiation of foreign debts by the Bolsheviks (10 February) had provoked a storm of protests and threats from the West. Nor did the Allies trust the Bolsheviks or sometimes even their own men, some of whom were suspected of having become too close to the Bolsheviks. The disruption of communications – it sometimes took telegrams up to a week to reach their destination, the interception of messengers, the confusion of languages and cultures all took their toll on relations between the small groups that controlled the destinies of nations and the fate of empires. Equally problematic were the various sources of information that came out of Russia. The British, for instance, had three different missions in Petrograd feeding information to London, and furthermore as no Allied government had recognized the Bolshevist state, all communications were unofficial. However, the Germans had recognized the Bolshevik government and on 23 April Count Wilhelm von Mirbach had arrived in Moscow as ambassador to the new Russia. As if to create further confusion amongst the Allies the unofficial French representative to the Bolsheviks hated the French ambassador based in Vologda, who was himself violently opposed to the Bolsheviks. Additionally, the USA was undecided as to its Russian policy but certainly was not in favour of allowing Japan to increase its presence in Siberia. Whilst schemes and plans were discussed and discarded events overtook the actions of the statesmen and politicians.

The Czech Legion, strung out along the 9,600km of the Trans-Siberian Railway, was subjected to an order disarming them on penalty of death. This order was issued by Trotsky on 25 May and went out to all Soviets along the railway. As soon as the Czechs realized what was afoot they took counter-measures and fought back. In rapid succession Penza, Chelyabinsk and Irkutsk fell into their hands. But they were not alone in several of these ventures as aid was forthcoming from anti-Bolshevik groups in the areas concerned, and they rapidly picked up the reins of power abandoned by the Bolsheviks who often fled with unseemly haste. However, the Red Guards still controlled the vital Baikal Tunnels, some 200km long, the destruction of which would cause havoc. Not wishing to isolate themselves from their escape route, the Red Guards blew only one section before they were routed by the Czechs and the railway was repaired by early August.

On 30 May martial law was proclaimed in Moscow. The Bolshevik secret security police, known as the Cheka and formed in late 1917, let it be known that the Cadet Party was behind the Czech revolt. It also encouraged the Germans to advance beyond Ukraine into Russia and helped anti-Bolshevik officers travel to the Volga and northern Caucasus regions in order to recruit for the Volunteer Army and the at the time more potent threat of General Krasnov's Don Cossack Army. This news was spread through the pages of *Izvestia*, the official newspaper of the Soviet government, and gained widespread credence.

Elsewhere events were spinning out of Lenin's control. In an attempt to suborn the SR's influence amongst the peasantry Lenin had, on 11 June, established the Poor Peasants' Committees which were intended to spread class war into the countryside by dividing the peasantry into groups. On the one hand, the poor peasants, on the other the rich, popularly known as Kulaks who were immediately thrust into the ranks of the counter-revolutionaries. An additional decree, dated 14 June, was issued from Moscow excluding SRs, other Left SRs, from Soviets across Russia.

As Krasnov's army of roughly 40,000 men with over 100 guns set about clearing the Don region of Bolsheviks and with the Germans in Rostov, Taganrog and the industrial region of the Don the VA had little scope for action. Consequently, it was decided to clear the northern Caucasus. However, it was Tsaritsyn (later Stalingrad) that was the focus of attention during the early summer of 1918. The city commanded the easily navigable Volga River as well as rail links to the Caucasus and Ukraine. The loss of Tsaritsyn would isolate the remnants of the Caucasian Army from Russia itself as well as the oil and foodstuffs of the region.

However, much had changed across Russia by the time the Czechs had the Trans-Siberian Railway operating again. It was as a result of the Czech's revolt that the first anti-Bolshevik, as opposed to nationalist, regime emerged. Samara, on the left bank of the Volga River was occupied by a Czech unit on 8 June. A local SR cell immediately formed a Committee of Members of the Constituent Assembly known by the acronym Komuch and an armed force called the People's Army under the leadership of Colonel V. O. Kappel. To the north-east in Siberia Omsk was the site of another SR coup and this resulted in the formation of the Provisional Government of Siberia, which proceeded to form its own army around a nucleus of former officers. Furthermore, it dissolved the soviets and restored private ownership of land and trade much to the disgust of the less right-wing politicians under its umbrella.

To avoid being subordinate to Komuch by dint of the latter's claim to be the new Russian government, it declared Siberia independent, complete with a green and white flag (symbolizing forest and snow) but with undefined western borders, on 4 July. Unfortunately, none of these anti-Bolshevik groups threw up a leader strong enough to unite their efforts. Even as Komuch came to power and the VA was about to embark on its summer campaign, the SRs of the People's Army informed Denikin's representatives that 'the VA will bring us dissent and we must therefore avoid merging with it'. Nevertheless, despite their discord the Greens of Siberia and Samara, the Whites of the VA and the Don Army all expanded the territory under their control. Ufa, Simbirsk and in August Kazan all surrendered to Komuch's forces. When Kazan fell into its hands so did the Russian state's gold reserve, some 650 million gold roubles, or in present-day values £25 billion. If it lacked allies, Komuch did not lack the funds to wage war.

The Czech revolt and Lenin's decision to rely on German good faith by not intervening in internal Russian affairs effectively opened one door for Allied participation in a renewed Russian Front, supported by the newly emerging anti-Bolshevik, pro-Allied governments in Siberia and Samara. Lenin did not want Allied aid through northern Russia or anywhere else but the Allies were determined upon it, the final act being the USA's agreement to support the Czechs, which came on 6 July. That same day the Murmansk Regional Soviet, lacking military force of its own, signed an agreement with General Poole that permitted the Allies to land up to 5,000 troops and occupy Archangel. Both ports were under British control by mid-August. To the south, Allied support was lacking when a shadowy body known as the Union for the defence of the Motherland rose against the Soviet in Yaroslavl, 250km north-east of Moscow. Similar uprisings took place in Rybinsk and Morom, home to Red Army munitions dumps and army groups HQ respectively. Only Yaroslavl remained out of Bolshevik control for more than 10 days, however. On 6 July the German ambassador was assassinated in his Moscow embassy by Left SR members of the Cheka. Suddenly Moscow itself was under threat from the Left SRs who were convinced that Lenin was bent only on destroying opposition to himself in Russia. Unfortunately for themselves, the Left SRs had not reckoned on the loyalty of the Latvian Rifle Regiment that garrisoned the capital. Within 48 hours Moscow was secure again but across Russia civil war was raging, the battle lines clearly drawn.

Self-proclaimed General G. M. Semenov. A former Cossack Staff Captain turned recruiting officer for the Provisional Government in eastern Siberia, Semenov fought against the Bolsheviks in early 1918 from his base in Manchuria. Briefly courted by the British who saw him as a means to counter Bolshevik recruitment amongst Austro-German POWs in this region at this time, he was a significant cause of Trotsky's mistrust of the Allied intervention. When he was dropped by the British Japan became his backer.

German troops land in Finland on 3 April 1918. Fears that they would march from there to Helsinki and Murmansk prompted British concerns for the Baltic Sea Fleet and the vast supply dumps at Archangel and Murmansk.

In response to the Czechs' reaction to the incident of 14 May Trotsky ordered that they be disarmed and in cases of refusal shot. They reacted swiftly and seized virtually every town and city of any importance along the Trans-Siberian Railway. Here Legionaries settle into a defence line outside of Omsk.

Kalmyck cavalry on parade. A Buddhist formation in the Don Army, the Kalmycks had been renowned horse breeders until their stock was confiscated by the Red Guards when they retreated from the Don territory in the spring of 1918. Such actions left bitter memories in the minds of the region's population.

Typical Cossacks of the Don Army. Germany wanted the Don region as a satellite state and Krasnov wanted to trade food for German munitions. This arrangement worked quite well until the Central Powers withdrew. The Don Army besieged Tsaritsyn without support from the VA. Krasnov's forces were unable to take this vital city.

Having rebuffed offers of cooperation from the Don Army, the VA embarked upon the Second Kuban Campaign on 23 June. Although a small force, the VA consisted of many veteran troops including a high percentage of officers that were well disciplined and highly motivated. One of the core units was the Kornilov Shock Regiment. It proved its worth time and again during this campaign.

General S. L. Markov, one of the heroes of the VA who was killed in action at Shablievka station whilst capturing an armoured train at the beginning of the Second Kuban Campaign. During this period the VA increased hugely in size and morale due to the successes it enjoyed.

Hetman P. P. Skoropadsky (right), Germany's puppet ruler of Ukraine, meets with Field Marshall von Hindenburg (left) in 1918. Skoropadsky ruled Ukraine from April to November 1918. His forces supported the troops of the Central Powers in suppressing nationalist aspirations and peasants opposed to the food requisitioning system.

The VA faced the retiring troops of the Caucasian Army. Of these the Taman Army proved to be the toughest opponent. Veterans of three years of campaigning against the Turkish Army, these men joined up with the main Red Army force on 18 September 1918. It was engaged in heavy fighting in the Stavropol region that autumn.

Leaving for war in 1918 a Kuban Cossack, fully equipped, bids farewell to his son. A large percentage of the VA's cavalry was made up of men such as this who had experienced the realities of Soviet rule and preferred other forms of government. However, the Kuban Rada (government) proved so unruly that in early 1920 it was dissolved by Denikin.

Officers and officials of the Don and Volunteer armies in Novocherkassk, capital of the Don lands. During the campaigns of 1918 there was little cooperation between the two forces due to General Krasnov's closeness to the Germans.

During the early hours of 17 July the Tsar and his family were executed by local Bolsheviks in the city of Ekaterinburg. Seen here in happier times, the executions were, in the words of Trotsky, needed 'to frighten, horrify and dishearten the enemy, but also ... to shake up our own ranks, to show them that there was no turning back, that ahead lay either complete victory or complete ruin'. As it spread, the news was greeted with a mixture of scepticism, sadness or indifference. No serious attempt to rescue the former royal family had been made.

On 8 October the soul of the VA, General M.V. Alexeyev died. The son of an ordinary soldier, Alexeyev had risen to the Supreme Command of the Russian Army on his own merits. His death caused Denikin to assume civil and military command of the VA. The complexity of the former task was too much for him.

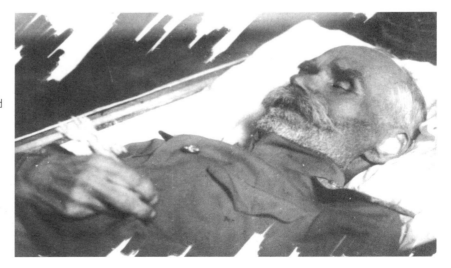

A mass grave. During the civil war all sides resorted to acts of mass murder as a means of creating order in their rear areas. The Red Terror was officially announced on 2 September 1918 in response to the assassination of the Cheka leader in Petrograd and the attempt on Lenin's life on 30 August. The announcement included the all-embracing sentence 'to be shot, all persons, touching the White Guard organizations, conspiracy and rebellion'. No other organization was as forthright.

Men of Komuch's People's Army fishing. Instead of a cap badge the men wore the orange and black stripes of the St George's cross. Indecision regarding an advance on Moscow, suspicion of other anti-Bolshevik groups as well as the lack of volunteers to fill its ranks led to the failure of Komuch and its army.

L. D. Trotsky (centre), the creator of the Red Army, addresses new recruits in late 1918 outside the Bolshoi Theatre in Moscow. From the date of his appointment as the chairman of the Revolutionary Committee of the RSFSR on 6 September 1918 he visited almost every front where his men fought, travelling in an armoured train. He introduced firm discipline at a time when such methods were frowned upon by many of his subordinates.

An armoured train of the Caucasian Army. Such trains provided invaluable mobile fire support for the far-ranging operations of all sides. The VA captured many such weapons systems during their North Caucasian campaign. Some were purpose-built leftovers from the First World War, others locally extemporized.

Red Army infantrymen, recruited from members of the Bolshevik Party. In possession of many armament factories and having inherited considerable quantities of munitions, the Red Army was well equipped from the beginning. What it lacked was experience, which was to be hard bought during the course of the early campaigns.

Under fire the crew of a Red river gunboat duck for cover. As well as the railways the great rivers such as the Volga, Don and Dnieper were hard fought for. During the Don Army's attempts to capture Tsaritsyn river gunboats provided artillery support as well as running in munitions and reinforcements.

By the end of 1918 the Trans-Siberian Railway was completely dominated by the Czech Legion. This vital artery ran through mountains and forests as well as crossing thousands of kilometres of uninhabited wilderness. Here Legionaries watch over a train derailed by partisans of indeterminate loyalty who were to grow in strength and audacity.

Chapter Four

Confusion be their Epitaph

When viewed with the hindsight of almost a century the subterfuges, ill-informed policies and ultimately pointless intervention of Britain, France, the USA, Japan, Greece and Italy appears to be selfish, contradictory, thoroughly confused and futile. The revolution of March 1917 replaced the Tsar with an apparently liberal, semi-constitutional government that superficially resembled that of Britain and France. Indeed, the removal of the Tsar's autocracy made the USA's entry into the First World War easier as the Provisional Government was a more acceptable ally than the Romanovs. When President Wilson addressed the Congress to call for war on 2 April 1917 the only Allied power other than Belgium to be mentioned in his speech was Russia, which he described as 'democratic at heart' and 'a fit partner for a League of Honor'. The Provisional Government was committed to continuing the war but Allied belief in its ability to do this began to wane as 1917 drew on. German propaganda, mainly directed at the British, dwelt at length on the Allied desire to fight to the last drop of Russian blood. Allied counter propaganda failed to rally much support and Russian war-weariness increased. However, whatever the activities of the Central Powers behind the lines the reports reaching London and Paris were, following the dismissal of Kornilov, increasingly pessimistic. Therefore, plans were made to bolster the Russian Front and prevent troops being transferred to the West and to Italy. Following the Bolshevik coup of November 1917, Britain and France divided southern Russia into zones of influence, Britain taking responsibility for the Caucasus and the Caspian Sea, France southern Ukraine, Crimea and the industrial Donbass region. At the time the purpose of this intervention was to encourage local forces such as the Don Cossacks, Ukrainian nationalists and Caucasians to oppose the Germans, Austrians and Turks as the Bolsheviks strove for peace. Initially, these were diplomatic moves with financial support and the promise of troops in the future when circumstances permitted. However, these efforts were not conceived as an anti-Bolshevik movement certainly in the early days. It was to protect the large Allied munitions dumps at Murmansk from the Germans that 500 British marines were landed in March 1918 under the command of Major General Maynard. A similar force arrived at Archangel in July led by General Poole. Both areas were now safe from German occupation with defensive screens established 200–300km down the railway lines and the inhospitable terrain itself doing the rest. But in the four months between the two events Moscow's attitude had changed from one of co-operation to one of confrontation. Poole was particularly eager to confront the Bolsheviks if the Allied governments were unwilling to recognize them. Merely to ignore them, Poole reasoned, would only generate hostility.

Neither course of action was taken. The Archangel landing was declared by Lenin to be 'a hostile act' and the local Bolsheviks were ordered to resist the Imperialists. As Red forces in the region were almost non-existent and French and American reinforcements had begun to arrive, the Bolsheviks fell back. However, as local support for the Allies was singularly lacking their attempts to advance came to nothing. By the end of the year roughly 35,000 Allied troops with a handful of Russians were defending the ports.

President Wilson's sanctioning of American intervention in the north and the east was bound up with his desire to contain Japanese expansionism in the far eastern provinces of Russia, as well as facilitating the evacuation of the Czech Legion. The Japanese had been the first to land men in Vladivostok. Of all the Allied activities the placing of their forces under Japanese command in eastern Siberia was possibly the most short-sighted. Russians of whatever political grouping mistrusted the Japanese thoroughly. The American commander in Siberia, General Groves, adhered strictly to Wilson's order not to intervene in Russian affairs, whereas the British chef du mission, General Knox, was firmly anti-Bolshevik. However, as Knox could raise only 1,500 men his power was limited to fighting Green and Red partisans. The French, led by General Janin, took the lead in western Siberia, incorporating the Czech Legion's 60,000 men into his command along with 12,000 Poles and 1,000 French troops.

Allied efforts in Siberia were frequently negated by internal rivalries, national aspirations and the conflicting orders received from their political masters. The latter often basing their decisions on out of date intelligence, rumour, speculation or pure wishful thinking. In the main they confined their activities to securing the rail network, warding off partisans and bandits and speechifying. But in south Russia matters were somewhat clearer.

French troops landed in Odessa on 18 and 25 December 1918 under General d'Anselme, followed by two Greek infantry divisions in early 1919. However, Denikin had been promised considerably more by the French Military Mission to the AFSR; unfortunately for him, Paris was no longer keen to commit its war weary and increasingly mutinous men. Equally confused were the Ukrainians who lent the French only grudging support as they appeared to have colonial ambitions in the area.

Lacking local support and distracted by conflicting ideas as to why they were there, the French and Greeks were defeated by the Red Army and abandoned the immediate area in early April and Crimea later that month. The former Dowager Empress and her retinue were evacuated in April 1919 aboard HMS *Marlborough*.

The British mission to the AFSR did not provide troops but supplies and instructors in quantity. Although some 500 instructors had arrived by early 1919, many lacked interest and only wished to go home. But, with the command passing to Major General Holman during the spring of 1919, British efforts took on a more professional aspect and training began in earnest on tanks, guns and trench weapons such as mortars. Artillery pieces, armoured vehicles and aircraft arrived at Novorossiysk in large quantities and were passed on to the elements of the AFSR. Again though ambivalence towards the AFSR in London prevailed and by April 1920 the British Military Mission had withdrawn. Wrangel's Russian Army was abandoned to its fate. Only in the Caucasus did the British mount serious operations in defence of the oil-rich Caspian Sea provinces which were under threat from the Ottoman Turks.

Led by Major General Dunsterville, British and Imperial troops occupied Baku in August 1918. Besieged by the Turks, the British evacuated the city on 14 September only to return in mid-November when the Turks sued for peace. In a strange little campaign the Royal Navy contested control of the Caspian Sea with Red gunboats based in Astrakhan. On the eastern shore of the Caspian an Indian Army force sent up from Persia under Major General Malleson supported anti-Bolshevik Moslems in Turkestan from August 1918 until April 1919. Malleson's force was withdrawn when the threat to India from the phantom armies of POWs did not materialize and the need for a re-generated Eastern Front had definitely become redundant with the end of the First World War. Furthermore, Turkish ambitions in the area had proved ephemeral.

Indeed, the collapse of the Central Powers and their evacuation of Russian territory made what had been the Allies' main reason for sending troops to the inhospitable north and south of Russia purposeless. Support for Kolchak and Denikin had outlasted the First World War and by mid-1919 was becoming a distinct political embarrassment. The people of the Allied states had no interest in Russia. Indeed, in many countries there was a feeling that such expeditions were immoral despite lurid tales of Bolshevik atrocities, and intervention was hurriedly wound down.

No Allied power had definitely committed to an anti-Bolshevik stance despite rhetoric that suggested otherwise to White, Nationalist or Green leaders. Operations in Siberia revolved around the Czech Legion and, as it moved towards Vladivostok, the bulk of the Allied troops went with them. Between November 1919 and April 1920 the majority of the Allied forces had left Russian soil. The Japanese finally retired in 1922 as their theatre of interest switched to China.

Although the Bolsheviks made much of Imperialist intervention, in reality its effects were negligible. Individuals such as Knox may have been rabidly anti-Bolshevik but there were few voices like his that were taken seriously. The diversity and confusion of Allied aims and the conflicting aspirations of the anti-Bolsheviks in Russia and abroad were too dissimilar for them to have coincided effectively. As Trotsky put it, 'Lloyd George is like a man playing roulette and scattering chips on every number'. It was an accurate portrayal of the Allies lack of policy. The USA's Secretary of State for War, Newton Baker, expressed many Allied statesmen's attitude when he said of Bolshevism, 'I don't like [it] . . . but . . . if the Russians like it, they are entitled to it'. Supporting the fledgling Polish and Baltic states was much more to France and Britain's liking and the Americans were happy to prevent Japanese domination of far eastern Russia. These aims were achieved as resentful Greens, Whites and Nationalists sailed or rode off into exile in the wake of their reluctant, confused patrons, whilst the Red flag was run up in Archangel, Sevastopol and Baku and along the length of the Trans-Siberian Railway to the Pacific coast.

A British Stokes mortar and crew, part of the British North Russian Expeditionary Force in Murmansk, during 1919. Allied troops held the line until replaced by local forces. On their left shoulder is the Polar Star badge.

Russian conscripts and officers in British uniforms. Their commander from January 1919 to February 1920 was General E. K. Miller. By the autumn of 1919 his force numbered 50,000 men, although many were unreliable and prone to mutiny and desertion. Miller went into exile when Murmansk fell on 21 February 1920.

Transport away from the railways was by sledge. Here sledges are loaded from a supply train south of Murmansk. The Allies evacuated the Arctic ports before winter set in.

Major General Ironside (second left) with a group of senior Russian officers. He appears to be speaking to General E. K. Miller. Ironside replaced Poole in October 1918.

American troops disembark at Vladivostok. They began to arrive on 10 August 1918. The American Siberian Expeditionary Force was made up of men from 8th Infantry Division plus 27th and 31st infantry regiments, numbering roughly 9,000.

Japanese nurses pose for the camera at a hospital in Vladivostok. The Japanese had begun to land in August 1918 and by November their numbers had increased to 72,000, rising to over 120,000 by the autumn of 1919. They provided much support for rogue Atamen such as Semenov and Annenkov, whose vicious, sadistic behaviour did much to polarize opinion against the Whites.

Lieutenant Colonel John Ward MP commanded the 25th Battalion Middlesex Regiment from beginning to end of the intervention in Siberia. A left-wing Member of Parliament and Trades Union organizer, Ward was a supporter of the proposed Constituent Assembly and later wrote, 'There was at once a clear issue – the Terrorist at Moscow, the Constitutionalist at Omsk. Had the Allies at this juncture translated their promises into acts, from what untold suffering Russia and Europe might have been saved!'

Czech Legionaries in Vladivostok waiting for repatriation to Europe, the last leaving on 2 September 1920. One Legionary who attained international fame was the author of *The Good Soldier Švejk*, Jaroslav Hašek. Hašek defected to the Red Army but in 1920 returned to Czechoslovakia, where he was regarded as a traitor.

Commanders (officers) and other ranks of the People's Revolutionary Army of the Far Eastern Republic. This Red Army formation was created in late 1921 to stamp out White and Green partisans and oversee the Japanese withdrawal.

German POWs in Siberia or Turkestan during the Russian Civil War. It was men such as these who were one of the root causes of British intervention. Indeed, many thousands of POWs enlisted in the Red Army usually in 'International' formations. Officers such as these were rarely welcome as they represented the bourgeoisie.

An American camp near Vladivostok. According to Colonel Ward, Kolchak had serious misgivings regarding members of the American force. The problem revolved around a number of translators who he knew to have been exiled from Russia for subversive activities but who had returned as American citizens. Kolchak did not trust their motives.

Men of the French 176th Infantry Regiment wait to disembark at Odessa. Several Renault tanks were landed at Odessa, one of which was captured by the Reds at the Battle of Berzovka in early 1919. The subsequent evacuation led to a period of 'Red Terror' in the city that cost thousands of lives.

A Turkish artillery position outside Baku during the summer of 1918. Turkish attempts to organize a pro-Ottoman consensus in the region fell on generally deaf ears. Following the British re-occupation of the city they retained troops in the area until 24 August 1919.

Sailors of the Red Navy's Caspian Sea flotilla. These men fought a campaign against ships officered and manned by the Royal Navy. When the British withdrew to Persia the Caspian Sea came under Red control.

British equipment did not only provide aid for the Whites but captured or war surplus passed into Bolshevik hands. Here a British-built DH 9a returns from a mission.

V. I. Lenin, the Bolshevik leader. He was happy enough to take 'potatoes and guns from the bandits of Anglo-French imperialism' when it suited but never regarded the Allies as anything more than invaders with regimes ripe for destruction.

General Baron Wrangel (facing the camera) on the deck of HMS *Benbow* in Istanbul harbour, late 1920. Exile was the fate of the luckier Whites and Greens.

Chapter Five

Black, Red, Green and White – the Rainbow at War

The summer of 1918 had witnessed the arrival of large numbers of Japanese, American, British and French troops in Vladivostock. The British, supported by Imperial and American forces, had also occupied Murmansk and Archangel. In these areas as well as on the Volga, where Komuch's writ ran, the clocks had been turned back to the days before the Bolshevik revolution of November 1917. Private ownership had been re-established, though not without resistance from those who had benefited from its nationalization, some of whom began to slip away into the forests and backwoods of Siberia and Central Asia from where they would begin to fight a partisan war. Even the politically disinclined Volunteer Army had been galvanized into issuing a more detailed policy statement – the Provisional Statute – which restored all laws and thus property rights to the position maintained before the Bolshevik takeover. Alexeyev's Special Council was becoming more military in its composition and singularly lacking in creativity. However, as the military situation in the North Caucasus was of paramount importance such matters, it was felt, could be left in abeyance for the while. Although grossly outnumbered, the VA had enjoyed a very successful summer's campaign that was to continue into the autumn.

Elsewhere, the Green Guard in the shape of Komuch was finding the Red Army a somewhat tougher nut to crack than originally anticipated. With Czech support the so-called Volga Front was constituted and was to be the foundation stone of the new Russian Front which would, so it was imagined, drive the Germans out of Ukraine. To Komuch's rear the Orenburg Cossack Host under Ataman General A. I. Dutov had also risen up and taken Orenburg, cutting Bolshevik Turkestan off from Moscow. However, what concerned the Red Army was the Volga Front, particularly those Komuch forces that were bolstered with and trained by Czech units of the Legion's 1st Division. Unfortunately, the People's Army lacked officers as many had left for the promises of better pay and advancement under the PGAS, as it now styled itself. Ranged against Komuch, Trotsky deployed the Eastern Army Group consisting of, from north to south, Third, Second, Fifth and Fourth armies, numbering roughly

70,000 men. It was the signing of a commercial treaty with Germany on 27 August that allowed Lenin to sanction the deployment of such major Red Army units to face Komuch. On 8 September Kazan was recaptured and two weeks later Samara besieged. As the People's Army fell back a conference was held in Ufa to debate the form of government that would rule until elections for a new Constituent Assembly could be held. With the People's Army collapsing and the Czechs withdrawing northwards, Komuch was forced to join the newly instituted All Russian Provisional Government, or as it became known the Directory.

The newly formed Siberian Army was commanded by General V. G. Boldyrev and numbered 30,000–40,000 men. The Allies had contacted the VA's General Alexeyev urging him to take command of the Siberian Army and thus unite the anti-German, anti-Bolshevik forces into a White/Green alliance. However, Alexeyev was unacceptable to either the SRs or their Czech allies.

Boldyrev's first task was to stabilize the front as the People's Army was all but encircled. As his men enabled the People's Army and other anti-Bolshevik forces in the area to escape capture, so the Directory bickered as to the division of authority in Siberia. During October Komuch was downgraded to a regional government, albeit at a distance despite a return to fighting form by a reinvigorated People's Army. Equally successful in driving back the Red Army, units of the Siberian Army were advancing on Perm. However, it is important to remember that the bulk of the fighting took place close to railway lines and was carried out by scattered formations, therefore a local victory could easily mean an advance of 50km or so to the next defensible railway station. This successful counter-attack was the opportunity that right-wing officers in Omsk had been waiting for. During the night of 17/18 November Admiral A. V. Kolchak, the Directory's Minister of War, became ruler of the Greens in Siberia with the magnificent title of Supreme Ruler. The socialist-inclined Czech Legion remained neutral but saved SR lives at the request of Komuch, now based in Ufa. On 30 November Kolchak issued Order 56 which authorized his army commanders to use force to crush Komuch activity. So much for an anti-Bolshevik coalition. However, with the First World War over the Allies were faced with a serious dilemma – how could they justify further action on Russian soil?

The Don Army made three attempts to take Tsaritsyn during the period August 1918–January 1919. Although the railway to the north and south of the city was cut and it was unable to send supplies down to the Caucasus, Tsaritsyn did not fall to Krasnov's Cossacks. The anchor of the Bolshevik's Eastern Front's right flank held firm. Stalin had arrived in the city to oversee the collection of food from the Caucasus but was held up there by the heavy fighting in that region. When Kazan fell to the Red Army Trotsky used the breathing space to create the Southern Army Group. The leadership committee of this front, Eighth, Ninth, Tenth and Eleventh armies, included

Stalin and C. E. Voroshilov, who almost immediately demanded the dismissal of General Sytin, the 'specialist' military expert appointed by Trotsky. Although Stalin appealed to Lenin, he received no support and other former Tsarist specialists were appointed.

Stalin was not alone in his opposition to a professional, regular army but Trotsky's vision of such a force was maintained and flourished for the rest of the civil war.

The Don Army's third failure before Tsaritsyn was symptomatic of deeper problems within the Don region. Fundamentally, the majority of Cossack troops were unwilling to fight beyond what they regarded as their borders. Once the area was cleared of Reds that was sufficient and they wanted to go home; this is precisely what they began to do at the end of 1918.

Having turned down the opportunity to support Krasnov's drive on Moscow in the summer, the VA had embarked on its own campaign in the northern Caucasus on 23 June. It was to prove one of the most remarkable operations in Russian military history. Denikin's 9,000 men were divided into 3 infantry divisions with roughly 3,000 cavalry, 21 guns and 2 armoured cars. Within three weeks the town of Tikhoretskaia, the lynchpin of the railway system not only in the Kuban but the entire Caucasus, fell into their hands. On 18 August Ekaterinodar, capital of the Kuban region, fell to the VA and the provincial government, the Rada, was installed. However, the Rada was to become a thorn in the side of Denikin's organization from that moment onward as its members were generally inclined to an independent Kuban, whereas the VA's policy was that of 'a united and indivisible Russia'. This was a slogan that played very badly to every nationalist group along the borders of the Russian empire. Following the capture of Ekaterinodar, the VA lost its purely volunteer status by introducing conscription, which increased numbers to some 35,000 by October. In the neighbouring Terek Cossack region and down to the Caucasus Mountains anti-Bolshevik revolts broke out. But even so Red Guard and the Bolshevized units of the retiring Caucasian Army still numbered over 60,000 men and were still capable of tenacious fighting. During the Ice or First Kuban Campaign few prisoners had been taken by either side. Later in 1918 POWs were a rich source of recruits for the Volunteer, Siberian, People's and Don armies. Indeed, once their commissars and commanders were eliminated, entire Red Guard and Army units changed sides. By the end of 1918 the VA had created a viable, prosperous and generally sympathetic base in Kuban and the northern Caucasus. It was the moment to look beyond mere survival. The Bolsheviks faced a grim new year with Kolchak in the east, Denikin to the south, the British and others to the north and with the collapse of the Central Powers' authority to the west and in Ukraine who knew what dangers from the Baltic States, Finland and the unknown quantity that was to become Poland. Even an atheist Christmas could not have looked bleaker.

The Second Kuban Campaign and the expansion of the VA led to the introduction of conscription. Here a group of Kuban Cossacks receive instruction in the use of the standard Russian machine gun, the Maxim model 1910.

A group of Bolshevik commanders avidly read bulletins or news sheets. The Red Army did not have officers as such but referred to its senior ranks as commanders. Each formation also included a Political Officer known as a Commissar. In the absence of uniform leather jackets and trousers were widely worn.

The fighting in Siberia was carried out by men such as these dressed in a mixture of old Tsarist uniforms with appropriate field signs, such as the green and white cockade of the Siberian Army and a strip of red cloth for the Red Army. Knowing who your enemy was almost a matter of which way you were facing, so much alike were uniforms.

There were more exotically dressed formations such as those seen here. These Semirechensk Cossacks under the command of Ataman Boris Annenkov wore a dramatic black uniform. A semi-independent warlord, Annenkov operated against Green and Red partisans in southern and eastern Siberia with extreme brutality.

On 23 November General Poole (saluting centre) and the British Military Mission landed at Novorossiysk to be greeted by Denikin (right). Denikin anticipated massive Allied support, including men as well as munitions.

Kolchak's forces had no cavalry equivalent to that of the AFSR. Here General A. G. Shkuro, one of the best known of Denikin's cavalry leaders, escorts his wife to the opening of a hospital named in his honour.

Away from the railways of Siberia the sledge was the main means of transport during the winter months.

A Bolshevik soldier at Tsaritsyn. Many were recruited from the non-Cossack inhabitants of the Don lands who were firmly behind any opposition to Krasnov's policies. The Tsaritsyn force was described by Trotsky as 'peculiar in its makeup [with] ill-disciplined commanders'.

As the industrial cities starved during 1918 the countryside was scoured clean by Bolshevik food-requisitioning parties that exacted harsh revenge on those who refused to part with their food stocks. Attempts to set richer peasant against poorer peasant gradually broke down community loyalty.

One of Kolchak's soldiers displays his St George's cross won for bravery. White leaders were split over awarding Imperial medals during a civil war.

One of the outstanding leaders of the VA during early 1919 was General, Baron, P. N. Wrangel (centre in dark attire). His abilities as a cavalry corps commander were outstanding. The Red Army had no similar force or leader. Tall, aristocratic and confident, he was nicknamed the 'Black Baron'.

During the final days of 1918 the Don Cossack Army began to disintegrate. As a Red Army report of December 1918 read, 'There is no question of reviving the old spirit of the Don, since their leader, Krasnov, does not have a broad base of authority.' Acting on this information, the Red Army attacked on 17 January.

At the heart of the VA were the three elite infantry units, the Kornilov, the Markov and the Drozdovsky regiments. Included in their ranks were many well-trained and highly motivated former officers who formed a tough kernel of anti-Bolshevik fighters.

The toughest opposition faced by the VA were the still organized units of the late Tsar's Caucasian Front. These men were fighting to get back to their homes in Russia as well as being anti-White Guard. They were hardened veterans with a clear purpose. It would take the VA months of hard fighting to eliminate this threat to its existence.

As the armies moved locust-like across the countryside it was the civilian population that remained to pick up the threads of everyday life. With their villages reduced to ashes and their young men conscripted by one side or the other, many took to the forests, marshes and mountains at first for safety but then as a base for fighting back.

The original metal red star cap badge of the Red Army was introduced in July 1918 and featured the worker's hammer and the peasant's plough. The plough was replaced by the sickle during 1919.

The standard Russian machine gun, the Maxim model 1910, was used by all sides during the civil war. Its robust construction made it virtually soldier proof and easy to maintain. This is an early model with the two supporting legs. The shield was often removed as its protective value was negated by its weight. The rate of fire was up to 600 rounds per minute.

The official entrance to the Tula arsenal during Imperial times. The Bolsheviks controlled much of the armaments industry in addition to inheriting huge stocks of munitions from the Provisional Government. Thus provided for, the Red Army began the civil war with a tremendous advantage over their opponents, who were much more reliant on captured or imported stocks.

Imported Chinese labourers that had entered Russia during First World War were stranded at the outbreak of the civil war. Many signed on with the Red Army. They gained a reputation as loyal, hard-fighting troops. They were regarded by Whites and Greens as ruthlessly cruel and treated with little mercy if captured.

A potential source of recruits for the Red Army was the POW camps scattered across Siberia and Central Asia, and this caused the Allies great concern. Although several thousand did join the Bolsheviks, the threat they posed was slight as such men had little or no interest in re-establishing the Russian Front. The majority just wanted to go home to central Europe.

Chapter Six

Adrift in a Counter-revolutionary Sea

January 1919 opened grimly for the Bolshevik regime. The collapse of German power had allowed Estonia to come under the control of a nationalist government that was prepared to oppose the Bolsheviks, the newly created Seventh Army of which was driven out with ease. This Red Army failure had created a dangerous enemy on the very doorstep of Petrograd.

Latvia's experiment with Bolshevism generated little support and a civil war broke out between German-sponsored nationalists and part of the Latvian Rifle Division. By May 1919 the fighting had ended, creating another anti-Bolshevik state. Lithuania, sheltered by a re-born Poland and its increasingly powerful army, settled under its own regime.

The Red Army followed the German evacuation of Belarus, steadily advancing towards the confused and controversial Russo-Polish borders. There was some skirmishing with the Poles but on balance the Bolsheviks were happy to concede ground rather than take on yet another enemy. Nevertheless, Trotsky ordered into being the Western Army to face the Poles and quell the insignificant Belarusian nationalist movement.

Ukraine, however, was a different matter; its food and raw materials were essential to the survival of the Bolshevik government, the power of which was confined to the Russian heartland. The German puppet ruler Skoropadsky had departed Kiev with his masters, thus leaving the way open for the return of the nationalists. Unfortunately, the rapid collapse of German and Austrian power left vast swathes of the countryside in the hands of local warlords commonly called Hetmens (not to be confused with Hetman Skoropadsky). The nationalist government known as the Directory had little hope of survival, lacking as it did much in the way of military muscle or support. When the Ukrainian Soviet Army crossed the border in January 1919 it trailed in its wake the new, embryonic Bolshevik Party of Ukraine's leadership. Over the course of the next three months the new regime spread its influence across the south and west of the country. However, any political control was but a veneer and the leader of the

Ukrainian Soviet Army became increasingly incapable of managing his ill-disciplined forces, crushing the Hetmen or completing the destruction of the nationalists. But the greatest threat lay in the grass-roots anarchist movement of the Makhnovist Insurgent Army that rode under the black flag of anarchy. Nestor Ivanovitch Makhno, a natural leader, had gathered around him peasants and deserters from various armies and caused trouble for the occupation forces as well as those of Skoropadsky. With the advent of the Directory, Makhno's band waited on events whilst keeping an eye on the border with Krasnov's Don region.

With the appearance of Bolshevik troops, Makhno was given command of Soviet forces in the Ekaterinoslav province. However, when he captured Ekaterinburg he argued with his masters and his forces were driven out. Unfortunately for the anarchists, there was no alternative but to align themselves with the Bolsheviks as the region under Makhno's control was threatened by units of the VA. Makhno's political programme was simple, 'to eliminate the Whites first and then the Bolsheviks' and to establish 'the People's Commune, the Anarchist Republic'. With 30,000 followers he was not a man to be trifled with by either side.

Across the entire sprawling canvas of the Russian Civil War there were dozens of groups similar to Makhno's. Hiding away in the forests of Siberia, central Russia or the marshes of Pripet, they fought against all comers. Some simply wanted a peaceful life, whilst others, frustrated by the lack of understanding of country life emanating from Moscow, Omsk or Ekaterinodar, fought for an ideal of freedom that was being eroded by the Bolsheviks, Whites and Greens. Official Soviet histories labelled Makhno's followers and their ilk bandits or counter-revolutionaries; he was one of many similar leaders who along with their forces would be used and then ruthlessly discarded when their value as extra bayonets diminished. In early 1919 Moscow had too many relatively powerful enemies ranged against it and therefore it was better to keep him close by.

Although the Red Army and its auxiliaries were surrounded by increasingly successful and aggressive adversaries, it had grown in size during late 1918 to just over 1 million men. Arming and equipping such a force was not difficult as the factories and arsenals, as well as huge stockpiles of weapons and clothing, were available to the Bolsheviks. Trotsky had, by early 1919, overcome the reservations of some of his comrades to increase the regular, professional nature of the army. With Lenin's support, discipline, similar to the ideas expressed by Kornilov in 1917, was enforced as was the establishment of hierarchical units from platoon to army corps. Indeed, the commander in chief was a former officer in the Tsar's army, the Latvian I. I. Vatsetis.

Luckily for the Bolsheviks, there were few organized internal enemies to deal with. There was the occasional bombing or assassination but quite simply the Greens and Whites were inept at organizing terrorist or partisan activities behind enemy lines. The attempt on Lenin's life in late August 1918 had been carried out by an SR acting alone. Besides which, Felix Dzerzhinsky's Cheka (effectively the secret police) was a relatively efficient and certainly brutal counter-espionage agency. In contrast, the VA, the Don Army and certainly Kolchak's regime in Siberia, now more White than Green, had to counter dozens of enemy groups behind their lines, be they nationalists, Left SR, anarchist or isolated bands of Bolsheviks. However, there was one White group, the so-called North Western Army, that had gathered around Pskov in late 1918 with German support that almost fulfilled this role. Numbering around 6,000 men, what it lacked was equipment and a leader to weld its feuding parties into a united formation. Such a man would appear in 1919 – the former Tsar's commander of the Caucasian Front, General N. N. Yudenitch. Yudenitch did not commit his tiny command to action prematurely, but decided to build up his forces and garner support before striking at the obvious target – Petrograd, birthplace of the revolution he so despised.

In only one area were the Bolsheviks enjoying real success, the Southern Front. Germany's withdrawal had left Krasnov's western flank completely exposed at the moment he had assigned the bulk of his forces to make the third attempt on Tsaritsyn. This last push failed and superior Bolshevik numbers drove back the Don Army across a wide front, indeed it was coming perilously close to collapse when Denikin offered a solution – a union of their resources.

Pressed by Eighth, Ninth and Tenth armies and with the large non-Cossack population (*inogorodnye*) seemingly supportive of the Bolsheviks, Krasnov had little choice. Even as the five weeks of negotiation ground on, the VA was in the process of destroying the reformed Eleventh and newly raised Twelfth armies and thereby clearing the Terek Cossack region and gathering up 150 guns and 50,000 POWs. On 15 February the Armed Forces of South Russia (AFSR) were created, comprising the VA, the Don Army and the Caucasian Army. Immediately, the 50,000-strong AFSR was under threat from five Bolshevik armies – fanned out from west to east, the Fourteenth, Thirteenth, Eighth, Ninth and Tenth armies, numbering upwards of 150,000 men. Led by General V. Z. Mai-Maevsky, the VA exploiting the rail network to the north of Rostov to its utmost and smashed any Bolshevik attempt to break through. On the right flank, running along the course of the Manych River, pressure from Tenth Army was increasing. However, a huge cavalry operation undertaken by the Caucasian Army broke the Tenth Army, which withdrew on Tsaritsyn. Having once again experienced the difficulties of life under the Soviet system, the Don Cossacks rose up behind Eighth Army and by June, in tandem with the reinvigorated Don Army, had disorganized and defeated Eighth Army, which began to retreat northwards.

Simultaneously, a small VA force broke out from Crimea adding to Thirteenth Army's difficulties, as elsewhere in Ukraine anarchists and nationalists were also moving against the Bolshevik regime and its army.

As Trotsky's Southern Front unravelled, the Eastern Front was also facing difficulties. The loss of Perm along with the collapse of Third Army was balanced somewhat by the recapture of Ufa and Orenburg. Whilst his men rested and waited for better weather, Kolchak introduced conscription. However, the increase in numbers was offset by the low quality and variable loyalty of many of the newly raised levies. These men were generally untrained and poorly motivated. This situation resulted in an offer from the British Military Mission to undertake their training and feed men into the army when they were ready. Unfortunately for Kolchak, this offer was shelved after a trial period. Kolchak's options were a direct march on Moscow, to link up with the AFSR in the south or the Allies in the north. In the centre was Gaida's Siberian Army, to its left General Belov's Southern Army, to the south of which lay the four divisions of Ataman Dutov's Detached Orenburg Army. Finally, holding the line to the Caspian Sea were 15,000 Ural Cossacks. The numbers were roughly even at 120,000 on each side but the Reds were stronger in machine guns and artillery. Furthermore, behind the White lines Red and Green partisans were operating in increasing numbers. Despite everything, the Whites recaptured Ufa and the Western Army had, by the end of April, advanced 550km. Elsewhere steadier progress had been made. With the coming of the thaw the White advance slowed to a crawl as the ground turned to liquid, bottomless mud and operations halted. The Eastern Front grasped the opportunity to regroup and Trotsky sent reinforcements. Had but Kolchak known it his advance had reached its zenith.

Estonia's armed forces were few in number but gave a good account of themselves. The unit seen here is the Partisan Battalion's machine-gun company. They are armed with a variety of weapons, including the Maxim 1910, Madsen light machine guns and a Lewis gun. The country carts behind were for transport. The men wore a death's head emblem on their left sleeve.

Latvia's cavalry favoured a German-style uniform, with the full dress version seen here. No Russian group supported Latvia's bid for freedom despite the loyalty of the Latvian Rifles to the Bolsheviks. As the Latvian nationalists battled to maintain their borders with British naval support they also fought a civil war against their own Bolshevik sympathizers.

Looking just like Germans, men of Prince Liven's Russian Army became a part of Yudenitch's Northern Army. Many had been POWs in Germany for several years and were unaware of the political upheavals that their homeland had undergone.

Men of Skoropadsky's army dressed in what was deemed national dress. These units dissolved in the wake of the German retreat, some men joining the nationalists of Petlyura, others the Whites, whilst some disappeared into the bands of anarchists and freebooters that roamed the Ukrainian steppe during 1919.

N. I. Makhno with his staff. Born in the village of Guilya Pole, he returned there after years of imprisonment for political activities. His relationship with Moscow was wary as he trusted the Bolsheviks only a little more than he detested the Whites. To Makhno all forms of authority endangered the liberties of the ordinary peasant or worker.

Mounting the Maxim gun on a country cart provided all sides in the civil war with mobile fire support. Makhno's forces were highly mobile and exploited the *tachanka*, as this weapon was known, to support their wide-ranging operations.

POWs. Prisoners were processed to weed out officers, commanders, commissars and deserters. Once this was done the rank and file were usually drafted into their captor's units. Sometimes they were split between companies, whilst at other times enlisted as entire formations.

Kuban Cossacks saddle up prior to going out on patrol. Traditionally, Cossacks slung their rifles over the right shoulder to distinguish themselves from other cavalry.

Many of the recruits for North Western Army were released POWs, such as the men seen here. Their motivation was questionable as they were returning to a country that had changed out of all recognition.

The 20th Armoured Car Company of the Red Army pose valiantly beneath their newly presented unit banner. During the First World War the Russians had made extensive use of armoured cars and continued to do so during the civil war.

Air power was increasingly important, although a lack of fuel and competent air crews limited the operations of all sides. These imported aircraft had been transported by rail to Vologda from the Archangel stores by the Bolsheviks. They are finished in clear dope and retain their Tsarist roundels.

Inside the lines at Tsaritsyn. The isolation of the city was never complete and the Soviet forces generally outnumbered and outgunned their opponents.

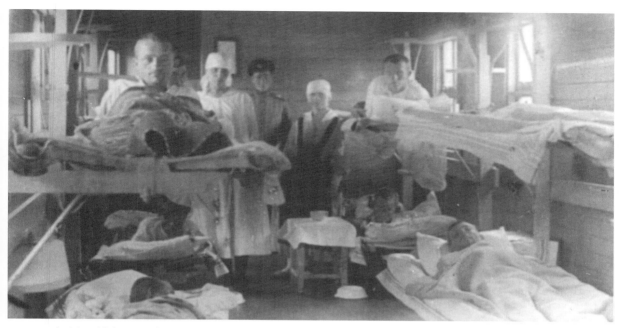

Inside a Volunteer Army hospital train. Those casualties lucky enough to be collected for evacuation to the rear enjoy the comfort of individual bunks. Medical facilities for all belligerents were often primitive in the extreme.

During the early months of 1919 British and French supplies began to arrive at Novorossiysk. However, not all items were suitable for local conditions or lacked parts, having been shipped from supply dumps across the Mediterranean and Middle Eastern theatres of operation.

From left to right, General A. P. Bogaevsky, who replaced Krasnov, Denikin, former Ataman P. N. Krasnov and General I. P. Romanovsky, Denikin's Chief of Staff. The photo was taken in Novocherkassk on the day the AFSR was formed, 15 February 1919.

Cossacks on the march during early 1919. Desertion prompted by Bolshevik promises of good treatment and amnesty undermined the Don Army's ability to stand against the Bolsheviks.

Czech General Rudolf Gaida resigned from the Legion and took command of Kolchak's Siberian Army in December 1918. His men's victory over the Third Red Army resulted in the capture of Perm, which provided 60 guns and almost 1,000 machine guns as well as 20,000 POWs.

As Siberian forces moved west, the Czech Legion retained control of the Trans-Siberian Railway and provided security forces to Kolchak's rear in co-operation with units from the Allied expeditionary forces. However, their remit was clear – to cover the line of evacuation for their own troops.

Weapons, such as this 122mm howitzer, captured during the spring campaign, enabled the AFSR to become more ambitious in its planning.

The banner of the artillery formation of the 1st Worker's Division, Red Army. Trotsky's persistence in making the Red Army a professional, disciplined force flew in the face of Bolshevik ideals, upsetting many of his comrades. However, experience and motivation were still lacking during the early months of 1919.

Chapter Seven

Zeniths and Nadirs – Target Moscow

The newly formed Armed Forces of South Russia (AFSR), under the command of Denikin, had originally planned to march on Tsaritsyn to link up with Kolchak's extreme left wing. But this was postponed by the Red Army's incursion into the Don lands. However, Mai-Maevski's masterful operations had dealt with that threat by the end of May and the AFSR had linked up with the rebellious Don Cossacks.

The AFSR now embarked upon a series of operations. The VA, with Terek Cossack support, took Kharkov, the Bolshevik capital of Ukraine and centre of a wide-ranging rail network on 27 June. Just three days later, with the support of British tanks, Tsaritsyn finally fell to the Whites along with 40,000 POWs and a mountain of supplies. To the Red Army's rear Ukraine was descending into chaos as several groups of their Green allies had turned against them. Faced with this horrendous collapse, Trotsky and Lenin reshuffled their assets and the first to go was the Commander in Chief Vatsetis, who was replaced in July by Kamenev. Stalin was ordered to Petrograd to stiffen the defenders' resolve against the increasingly aggressive activities of Yudenitch's North Western Army. It was now apparent that the greater threat to the Bolshevik government came from the AFSR and that Kolchak's Siberians could be dealt with later. Kamenev's plan involved splitting the advancing AFSR in the centre near Kharkov where the VA and the Don Army aligned. Unfortunately, for Trotsky Denikin had also planned a major operation which he was to reveal to his subordinates at Tsaritsyn on 3 July. It was known as the Moscow Directive.

The three major elements of the AFSR were to proceed as follows. The Caucasian Army would march on Saratov where it was anticipated it would link up with Kolchak's southern flank and then turn towards Moscow. The Don Army would head north passing through Voronezh and then Moscow, whilst the Volunteer Army was tasked with reaching Moscow via Kursk, Orel and Tula with its left flank covered by the Dnieper River, which it was ordered not to cross. The plan met with a mixed reception, notably from Wrangel who suggested that it would be better to re-group and organize the rear before driving on to the capital. After some discussion it was decided to continue with the original plan, capitalizing on the Red Army's disorganization, denying them the opportunity to regroup and thus maintaining the AFSR's momentum. Kamenev's counter-offensive of August held up the Don and Volunteer armies' plans, but by the end of July Wrangel's advance guard was within 100km of Saratov.

On 29 July Poltava fell and the VA advanced into Ukraine, taking Kiev on 30 August. But Kiev was a distraction, as was the seaborne operation that resulted in the occupation of Odessa. This further diluted the AFSR's order of battle, which was being stretched thinner by the day as the pace of the advance increased. The conscription of peasants and POWs did little to alleviate the AFSR's growing shortage of manpower, as one British observer put it, 'The quality of the infantry regiments . . . varied enormously . . . peasants . . . mobilized against their will and who were unintelligent and untrained in war. They were naturally poor.' He also commented on the terrain, 'The plains of south Russia favour the free movement of troops everywhere although there are few metalled roads . . . the main operations were confined, as a rule, to the vicinity of railways . . . with the exception of the rivers, there are no obstacles south of the forest belt'. However, he was particularly damning of Russian officers in general, regarding 'the majority of them to be corrupt and inefficient . . . they took no interest in the welfare of their men', even quoting one as saying, 'He is a peasant – he is nothing.' It was mainly by recruiting these 'nothings' that the VA had almost quadrupled in size to over 150,000 men. Many such were in training behind the lines or protecting the increasingly vulnerable railways which provided the only effective supply chain. As the AFSR advanced so did problems for the vast rear areas. Now only Tula stood between the VA and Moscow. Then the Red Army struck back. To the west of Orel Fourteenth Army drove a wedge between the Kornilov and Drozdovsky divisions, and to the east a large Bolshevik cavalry force engaged the Kuban Cavalry Corps of General A. G. Shkuro and Mamantov's Don Cossacks near Voronezh. Buddeny's I Cavalry Corps emerged victorious and to avoid encirclement the VA began to fall back. As it retreated the VA began to lose recruits in droves. Simultaneously, the black-flagged anarchist's of Makhno's incredibly mobile forces unleashed their own havoc behind Denikin's lines. As if from nowhere, Makhno's re-invigorated army burst into Denikin's rear in early October. Roaming about almost at will, the anarchists took the important railway station of Ekaterinoslav, even threatening Denikin's HQ and supply depot at Taganrog. This offensive forced Denikin to withdraw troops from the front to re-establish order. As the VA retreated south so did the Don and Caucasian armies, the latter falling back on Tsaritsyn on the extreme right flank.

With the onset of winter the high command of the AFSR retired on Rostov on

Don and watched with increasing nervousness as Kharkov and Kiev were lost during December. Gradually, losing cohesion, elements of the AFSR fell back into Crimea, others towards Poland. As military and refugee trains clogged up the lines, typhus began to spread through all armies. In January 1920 Tsaritsyn, Rostov and Taganrog all fell and the Don Army almost ceased to exist as many men simply went home.

Fighting continued throughout January and February, and although they inflicted heavy casualties, the AFSR was on the point of dissolution. Don and Kuban Cossacks began to desert in ever increasing numbers and Green partisan groups sprang up everywhere. Indeed, Green activity increased significantly along the Caucasian Black Sea littoral as local SRs attempted to create their own Black Sea republic. Although they entered into negotiations with the Bolsheviks, nothing but submission to the Red Army was offered to them. Nor were the Reds in much better shape. Commander M. N. Tukhachevsky took over the newly formed Caucasus Army Group just as it was decimated by typhus and short of supplies, with its rear consisting of little but devastation for hundreds of square kilometres. Regardless of this, the Reds launched a wide-sweeping cavalry attack led by First Cavalry Corps which turned the right flank of the AFSR. A last-ditch attempt to cut this off failed in the teeth of a blizzard. On 17 March, with the line of the Kuban River proving indefensible, Ekaterinodar fell and the VA with some Kuban and Don Cossack units fell back to the port of Novorossiysk. From there, amidst scenes of complete chaos, some 35,000 troops were evacuated to Crimea by the end of the month.

From Crimea Denikin left for exile, his place being taken by Wrangel. At least Denikin was alive, whereas Kolchak who had passed his title of Supreme Ruler to Denikin in January 1920 was a frozen corpse in the Angara River.

Kolchak's meteoric rise and equally rapid fall was a direct result of political and military failure. The Siberian SRs had clear instructions to overthrow Kolchak's regime dating from May 1919. The next step was to negotiate a truce with Moscow with the intention of creating autonomous regions within a federal Russia. From the SRs' perspective, the Bolshevik grip on power was weak and they hoped to set an example that would be followed elsewhere, thereby, so they anticipated, eroding Lenin's power base by political rather than military means. They did not know their enemy.

By the end of the Siberian thaw in May 1919 the Eastern Front was on the march again. Initially, Khanzin's Western Army received the main Red thrust, which burst through the gap between the Western and the Siberian Army on its right. Within six weeks the Whites had fallen back some 80km and lost their best reserve unit, the Officer's Shock Regiment consisting of some 3,000 veteran infantry, in an ill-judged assault on a partisan unit. Changes at the top did not improve morale and the conscripts deserted in their tens of thousands. The Reds crossed the Ural Mountains and Chelyabinsk and Ekaterinburg fell into their hands, opening the prospect of a rapid advance across the Siberian steppe. However, the Red Army was now over extended and a White counter-attack forced their enemies back. But by 15 October the Whites had been driven back to their start line and with winter approaching Kolchak's capital, Omsk, was in danger. Nor could Kolchak summon help as the Southern and Orenburg armies were in total disarray and fighting for their survival, as was the remainder of the Ural Cossack Host. Exhausted and divided by superior numbers, including large groups of Green partisans, the Supreme Leader's armies melted away. On 14 November Omsk fell and the Whites retired along the railway to Irkutsk, itself a SR stronghold. Having announced the formation of a new People's Army, hinting at a resurrection of Komuch, three days later Gaida led an abortive coup. Yet even as his regime crumbled, Kolchak refused to compromise with the Greens and, finally, when his troops broke an armistice brokered by the Allied missions in Siberia Kolchak surrendered and was tried and executed on 6 February 1920. But his death did not end the fighting. Many Green Partisan units allowed themselves to be absorbed into the Red Army when the end of the Whites seemed imminent. At the time it seemed logical but by losing their armed support the Greens had effectively forfeited any realistic hope of an SR-dominated Siberia.

October 1919 had witnessed the high point of Denikin's advance in the south and the revival of Kolchak's fortunes in the east. But to the north-west events had also reached a peak with Yudenitch's North Western Army overlooking Petrograd. Yudenitch had command of the NWA in the early summer of 1919 on Kolchak's orders. His brief was simple, with British, Estonian and Finnish help he was take Petrograd. The occupation of the scene of the Bolshevik's first triumph was anticipated to be a crucial turning point that would provoke spontaneous uprisings all over Russia, which in turn would sweep Lenin and his followers away. However, no substantial aid was forthcoming from Estonia and Finland who predicated any help with the requirement that their independence be acknowledged, which Kolchak was not prepared to do.

Nor were the British inclined to give White generals unconditional support without some form of liberal government being in place first. To this Yudenitch agreed. After a false start, the NWA's 30,000 men began their offensive on 15 August. On a 300km front they advanced through appalling terrain that, as usual in this civil war, confined operations almost exclusively to the railway lines. The right flank took Luga in early October and the left flank Yamburg as the Red Seventh Army fell back in disorder. By late October Petrograd was in sight as the NWA occupied the Pulkovo Heights. But other rail links to the east and south remained in Red hands and they were able to send in reinforcements. The counter-attack was launched on 21 October by Fifteenth Army, followed up by the restored Seventh Army, its ranks filled by Red Guards and Petrograd's workers. Within less than a month the NWA was back in Estonia thoroughly defeated. Riddled with typhus, Yudenitch's command was disarmed by the Estonians.

The year 1919 had ended and the Whites last hope for victory rested on the shoulders of Wrangel shut up in Crimea. Elsewhere in Russia, the Bolsheviks generally reigned supreme. It had been an incredible 12 months.

The AFSR's 1919 spring campaign was based upon efficient use of the rail network. Troops were shuttled back and forth, fighting where necessary with no front line other than railway stations. Armoured trains such as this one, the 'Ivan Kalita' commanded by Colonel R. R. Zhelenitsky, provided the mobile artillery support for such fast moving operations.

Aid from the AFSR to the Don insurgents was provided by means of an air bridge. Although small in number, the morale effect of the flights was immense. Here a Soviet anti-aircraft machine gun mounted on a *tachanka* attempts to bring down a supply plane.

The AFSR's victory parade through Kharkov featured this extemporized armoured car named 'Russia'. The roundel colours from the outer are red, blue and white as in the Russian tricolour.

As well as tanks, the British provided armoured cars such as these three Austin Mark 3s. Russian crew men and British instructors (probably in shorts) mix by their vehicles. When Denikin arrived in the city Wrangel quipped, 'Your Excellency we had a very rough time.'

Men of the AFSR's 7th Infantry Division dressed in British kit. The supplies sent by the British ranged from tanks and guns to medical supplies and saddles. Such dress convinced the Soviets that British troops were fighting with the AFSR. The machine guns are of Austrian manufacture.

Denikin (on foot with his back to the camera) declared his intention of marching on Moscow following a service of thanks at Tsaritsyn cathedral. Not all were supportive of this ambitious offensive, Wrangel amongst them.

A Red Army man, armed with a Japanese carbine and Russian grenades, relaxes in Moscow. With the capital under threat from Kolchak and Denikin, call-up papers went out to more and more classes of men.

A Red Army artillerymen with a 122mm howitzer. Possessing the factories that produced such weapons, and more importantly the appropriate ammunition, was a huge advantage for the Red Army.

Some of 'Shkuro's Wolves', the nickname given to men of General Shkuro's original unit of Kuban Cossacks. It came from the unit's standard which featured wolf pelts. They enjoyed a reputation for their ferocity and rabid anti-Bolshevism.

General K. K. Mamontov, leader of the division-sized cavalry raid behind Red Army lines. From 10 August to 19 September IV Don Cavalry Corps cut a swathe through Tambov province, destroying rail lines, stores and generally causing havoc. In the short term the rear of Trotsky's Southern Front was in turmoil, in the long run it achieved very little other than a mountain of loot.

The Bolshevik response to the AFSR's superior cavalry parade for their commander, S. M. Buddeny, a former NCO in the Tsar's army, were horsemen such as these troopers of I Cavalry Corps. The dress style was eccentric as every man turned out in what he had. Nevertheless, they proved to be a formidable fighting force.

Leaving Moscow for the Southern Front, the men who answered Trotsky's famous call, 'Proletarians to horse'. To combat the AFSR's superior cavalry Trotsky requested that the Red Army form cavalry units of its own.

Makhno (smiling) and a group of his closest supporters. Following a failed Bolshevik assassination attempt in May 1919, Makhno's attitude to them was ambivalent. However, his hatred of the Whites was unswerving. During the summer of 1919 his forces had fought running (often quite literally) battles in the rear of the AFSR.

When Novorossiysk was taken by the Reds British and other supplies were captured in huge quantities. These included tanks such as this one, which was salvaged from the harbour where it had been ditched. Thousands unable to find passage on the ships marched south along the coast.

Identifying friend or foe often depended on the favour sported. The red cotton stripe is all that shows the wearer to be a Red Army man.

One of Kolchak's conscripts. As the entire White line began to buckle, Kolchak replaced Gaida with General A. N. Pepelyaev, renamed the Siberian Army First Army and split the Western Army into Second and Third armies. The whole was commanded by General M. K. Dietrichs.

The remains of Denikin's air force in a workshop in Taganrog. A motley collection of aircraft was used by both sides during the civil war, but demonstrated, to those who cared to notice, the efficacy of air power when used for ground attack against troops exposed on terrain devoid of cover.

White POWs wait to hear their fate. Many men changed their allegiance several times as the 'poor bloody infantry' of all sides was regarded as mere cannon fodder to take an enemy bullet.

A British-supplied Whippet tank with a Russian officer. Although not a decisive weapon, its morale effect on an unsophisticated enemy was profound.

Wrangel's Konvoi (bodyguard unit) of Cadets parade in Crimea. Mainly dressed in British uniforms, these youngsters were devoted to the 'Black Baron'. Wrangel and Denikin had often disagreed over strategy, but with the AFSR's collapse the way was made clear for Wrangel's policies and ideas.

Chapter Eight

Crimean Sunset

Across the narrow neck, the Perekop, of the Crimean peninsula ran an old defensive line known as the Turkish Rampart. Roughly 15km long, it had been built to cover a man-made ditch that had, in the time of Turkish rule, flooded to create a moat. To the west a bridge connected Crimea to the Chongar Spit that ran out from the mainland, south of which lay a large area of tidal salt marshes. These lines had been occupied by General Y. A. Slashchev's forces retreating from Ukraine in late 1919 and held in increasing strength by the re-organized AFSR, now controlled by Wrangel under the name of the Russian Army. With Denikin gone, Wrangel's forceful personality had whipped his demoralized soldiers into a cohesive fighting force. Crimea had been relatively unscathed by the war and its Mediterranean climate and ample food supplies reinvigorated the new arrivals. However, Britain had effectively washed her hands of further intervention in Russia, and France's support was more verbal than practical. The USA was not interested in Wrangel only Siberia, where it maintained a watch over Japanese ambitions. Therefore, Wrangel was left to his own devices. Feelers were extended to find potential allies but only the Poles responded and they had their own agenda. On 24 April Polish troops crossed into Ukraine and by 6 May had occupied Kiev. The Polish attack merely pre-empted one that Moscow had been planning for several months. The Red Army's Western Front commanded by the ubiquitous Tukhachevsky, stood in Belarus, South Western Army Group (under Egorov) below the Pripet Marshes. Falling back before the Polish advance, Tukhachevsky struck back and by mid-August had reached the Vistula River close to Warsaw. A Polish counter-offensive, the Battle of Warsaw, drove the Red Army back almost to its start line. The possibility of carrying the 'World Revolution' into Eastern Europe had collapsed and peace was concluded on 12 October. The Russo-Polish War did little for Wrangel other than extend the lifetime of the 'Crimean Redoubt'. Although his Russian Army was rebuilt and broke out from Crimea to the mainland, its last months were a time of diminishing hope. Nevertheless, the Russian Army did fight on and achieved some success.

The reorganization undertaken by Wrangel split the army into three formations – the I Army Corps based around the three veteran divisions of the Volunteer Army,

II Army Corps the Don Corps and the Composite Cavalry Corps. It was this army that launched the last White offensive. Spearheading the attack with a handful of tanks, the I Corps broke through Thirteenth Army's Perekop defences. Having cleared the peninsula, the Whites advanced towards the lower reaches of the Dnieper River taking the city of Melitopol. In less than two weeks Wrangel's men had occupied much of the Tauride province, gaining vast stockpiles of much-needed food.

The Red counter-attack was not long in coming. I Cavalry Corps, led by a former miner, Commander D. P. Zhloba, in an attempt to cut the White lines of communication into Crimea rode to its destruction. Zhloba himself survived to face demotion, but as the scattered remnants of his corps passed into captivity, Cossacks focused on a valuable source of mobility and rounded up some 3,000 horses. However, despite the advance into the Tauride and the defeat of Zhloba, there was no significant uprising in the Don lands as a consequence. Therefore, it was to the Kuban lands that Wrangel turned next. Even as a force landed on the marshy shoreline of the Kuban where General S. G. Ulugai was to lead the population in a rising against Bolshevik rule, the Red Army had gained a foothold over the Dnieper River at Kakhovka. The Kakhovka Bridgehead was to prove an impossible nut for the Russian Army to crack. The Kuban expedition failed to spark a revolt, but did garner some thousands of recruits and Ulugai returned to Crimea before the end of August. And all this time Trotsky had been gathering his forces under the slogan 'all against Wrangel'. Aware of Bolshevik preparations, Wrangel ordered a pre-emptive attack, the so-called Trans Dnieper Operation, which, although marginally successful, did not disrupt the Red Army's assembly areas or eliminate the bridgehead. First Cavalry Army was tasked with cutting the Russian Army's line of retreat. With 130,000 men facing less than 40,000 and Commander M. V. Frunze recently arrived from the Turkestan Front, and under orders to disregard casualties, there could be but one outcome.

Southern Front unleashed its offensive on 28 October but failed to trap the Whites, who regained the Turkish Rampart during the course of the next four days. This temporary respite allowed Wrangel to put into operation his long-planned evacuation strategy. For months fuel had been stockpiled to enable a seaborne evacuation to Constantinople. On the third anniversary of the Bolshevik coup, 7 November, *Pravda*'s headline read, 'Forward again! No shrugging of the mighty shoulders. The hour of world victory is near.'

By 11 November the last major defence line at Iushun had been breached by the Latvian Division. As its rearguard units fought gallantly to stem the tide, Wrangel's armada, working to a strict timetable, picked up those chosen for evacuation – in all some 146,000 people. By 16 November the last ships had left. The Russian Army sailed into its exile and with it the last significant White opposition to the Bolshevik regime. On the previous day Frunze had officially announced the fall of Sevastopol, concluding with the words, 'The tortured country now has the chance to begin to heal the wounds inflicted by the imperialist and civil wars.' Or as Commander P. K. Mironov of Second Cavalry Army wrote, 'The last joyous rays of the sun witnessed the last volley from the Red artillery on 12 November 1920.'

Russia, or to give it the official name of the Russian Soviet Federated Socialist Republic (RSFSR), was in a terrible condition. The railways were almost inoperable and food was in short supply, particularly in the cities. Nor was Wrangel's defeat the end of armed opposition to the Bolsheviks. Faraway to the east of Siberia the remains of Kolchak's army had, in April 1920, been organized into 3 army corps of just over 20,000 men. This was carried out in Chinese Manchuria under the watchful eye of the Japanese. Although units of Makhno's army had taken part in the final battles in Crimea, he himself had stayed in his home town, Gulyai Pole, preparing for the Anarchist Congress in Kharkov later that month. Makhno did not attend, nor did the congress take place. The Cheka, with all the major anarchists in place, rounded them up and executed them on 26 November. Simultaneously, Gulyai Pole was surrounded by the Red Army. Makhno was lucky to escape, escorted by his 100-strong Black Guard. Gathering his supporters from nearby anarchist garrisons over the next few days, he led them to recapture Gulyai Pole. Usefully, the Makhnovist troops in Crimea escaped a Cheka trap. Frunze, under orders from Moscow, drew up a list of crimes, such as disobeying orders, to justify the hunting down and exterminating all who professed support for Makhno's policies. As the Ukrainian towns and countryside were crawling with Bolshevik troops, Frunze ordered, 'a concentric offensive from the northwest, the north and the east . . . to beat . . . the Makhnovist detachments . . . towards the Sea of Azov and ruthlessly exterminate them'. But, once again, as he had done with the Whites in 1919, Makhno delivered his pursuers a lesson in mobile partisan warfare.

Covering up to 80km per day, with his men all mounted or riding in *tachankas*, he evaded encirclement. With a hard core of some 2,000 men, Makhno traversed the eastern Ukraine striking at all forms of Bolshevik organization from local soviets to army staffs. To encourage anarchist uprisings elsewhere, messengers were dispatched to the Don area and Voronezh province, where they achieved some support. However, the end was inevitable as the Red noose tightened. With the last of his followers, Makhno made a 1,000km dash and crossed the border into Romania on 28 August 1921. Other partisan formations of varying political allegiances, be they Green, White, Black or nationalist, remained at large in both eastern and western Ukraine until 1924, but their efforts came to nothing. War weariness and the simple struggle to survive day to day had become the motivation that drove most of the population. Indeed, the same could be said of some units of the White armies at this time. Ataman Kalmykov, leader of the Ussuri Cossacks, one of several warlord-bands that had operated in eastern Siberia under the vague authority of Kolchak, was the victim of a mutiny by his own men.

The colour party of the Kornilov Division on its way to Crimea from Novorossiysk. When they disembarked one veteran remembered, 'the pier, parks and main streets were full of ladies in spring dresses . . . Brilliantly outfitted officers of rear formations'. Wrangel conducted what amounted to a purge of the rear echelons, cutting their establishments to the bone to fill the firing line.

Mounted scouts of the Kornilov Division. Lucky were the mounted troops who managed to find horses as many thousands had been abandoned or killed by their masters at Novorossiysk.

As the Bolsheviks possessed no naval forces on the Black Sea, Wrangel was at liberty to send ships to collect large numbers of Cossacks who had taken refuge near the Georgian border. This is one of Wrangel's sailors.

Sporting red star emblems, Russian armoured cars are transported westwards to face the Polish invasion. To the right is an armoured train with rudimentary camouflage, a response to the fact that aerial reconnaissance was becoming increasingly effective.

Zhloba's cavalry was subject to the attentions of Wrangel's small air force. Machines such as this Nieuport 11 were almost unopposed in the air. As Wrangel remembered, 'White aircraft came flying low, machine gunning and bombing the panicked cavalry'.

The banner of an unidentified Red Army formation reads, 'To smash Wrangel'.

Taking messages from officers in the new Red Army uniforms are Kalinin (Chairman of the Central Committee, with beard) and Buddeny (seated next to Kalinin). With the conclusion of hostilities with Poland all of the Red Army's resources could be concentrated against Wrangel.

Red Army men inside the Kakhovka Bridgehead pose for the camera along with their mascot and a 37mm trench gun. The fortifications erected to defend the bridgehead were heavily wired and provided with a significant number of guns to act as anti-tank weapons. Trotsky and his staff were well aware that the Whites would be unable to sustain a battle of attrition which is what the Reds were preparing for.

As the truce was signed with Poland, two cavalry and three infantry armies formed up in an arc facing Wrangel's forces. Amongst them was First Cavalry Army the Tachanka, which is seen here.

The ditch below the Turkish Rampart some 7 or 8m deep. To the left the wiring can be seen. The White defences on the left consisted of a trench system backed with artillery.

Armoured trains, such as the 'United Russia' seen here, were used to cover and transport the White rearguards as they fell back. Demolition teams destroyed track and bridges as they went.

Part of a panorama showing the storming of the Perekop by the Red Army. Under heavy fire from machine guns, rifles and artillery, wave after wave of infantry flung themselves down into the ditch and scrambled up the bank to face hand-to-hand combat.

Obsolete position guns formed part of the Russian Army's support for the trench lines at Perekop. The rail line was for the shell trolleys to carry the shells from the bomb-proof shelters to the left.

Red Army engineers pose by a tank captured at Kakhovka during the fighting of the summer. Although they were unable to use them in the Crimean fighting, such trophies would form the nucleus of the Red Army's armoured forces in the early 1920s.

The lighter defences facing the Shivash Marshes were breached when a freak combination of wind and tide lowered the level of water, thus allowing the Red infantry to wade across. This move outflanked the Perekop defences, although again casualties were high.

Red infantry parade and listen to motivational speeches before going into the line.

Clad in a variety of uniforms, men of the Russian Army assume a defensive pose for the camera. During the fighting in the Tauride Wrangel's troops often formed squares to hold off Red cavalrymen.

Colonel P. G. Buzun and his wife Adjutant V. I. Buzun. He was the last commander of the Alexeyev Regiment, one of the most famous units of the Volunteer and Russian armies. Her *cherkasska* has four wound stripes and she is wearing a soldier's St George's Cross alongside an Ice March badge. Women soldiers were not unknown on all sides.

General Baron R. F. Von Ungern-Sternberg, one of several White warlords who carried out partisan warfare in Siberia and all points east. Ungern-Sternberg had raised Mongolian troops and fought for an independent Mongolia, mixing mysticism with politics as well as fighting the Bolsheviks.

The captured flag of Makhno's forces. The slogan reads 'Death to whomsoever does not want to give freedom to the labouring people'.

Chapter Nine

Bolsheviks Triumphant

The year 1921 marked the official, Soviet, end of the Russian Civil War. As the borders with the Baltic States, Finland, Poland and Romania were settled so it remained for the Bolsheviks to deal with the Caucasus. The collapse of the Tsarist Caucasian Army had allowed the area south of the Caucasus Mountains to dissolve into three independent states, Georgia, Azerbaijan and Armenia, of which Georgia, homeland of Stalin, was the most powerful. Having enjoyed peaceful if sometimes problematic relations with the Kuban Rada and Denikin's regime, Georgia found itself faced with no buffer states between itself and Bolshevik Russia. By the spring of 1921 both Armenia and Azerbaijan were militarily impotent and therefore Georgian independence depended on the Georgian Army alone. Although nationalist fervour had created the Georgian republic, its politics were left wing of the Menshevik persuasion and therefore they were as unacceptable to the Bolsheviks of Moscow as the SRs of Siberia. Indeed, their position had been clearly laid out by their leader, 'We prefer the imperialists of the west to the fanatics of the east.' Following the evacuation of the AFSR from Novorossiysk, the Red Eleventh Army, supported by several armoured trains, took up positions on Azerbaijan's northern border. As Azerbaijan had no army to speak of and an increasingly vocal Bolshevik fifth column, when Eleventh Army crossed the border it took a mere five days to overrun the country. With the occupation of Baku oil could once again flow to the factories of Russia. Patiently, Lenin waited until November 1920 before taking similar steps in Armenia. By late January 1921 Armenia's farms were subjected to the same ruthless food-requisitioning policies that maintained across all Bolshevik territories. Now only Georgia remained, yet from fear of British intervention, Lenin refrained from invasion. When it became clear that Britain regarded the whole of the Caucasus as lying beyond its sphere of interest, the Red Army struck. Crossing the Caucasian Mountains during February was an unpleasant task but other units entered from Azerbaijan. The Georgian Army fought against odds of three to one and they were faced with veteran troops under experienced commanders. Nevertheless, the battle for Tiflis ended only with the arrival of strong reinforcements. The Georgian capital was occupied on 25 February 1921. Lenin, pleased to have restored Russian rule in another border area and particularly one blessed with such rich assets, counselled caution when dealing with the Georgians, '[local] Communists must avoid any mechanical copying of the Russian pattern'. Moscow was well aware of the passionate hatred the Georgians had for Russians whatever their political brand. Although the Caucasus was the scene of uprisings for years to come, none posed a significant threat to Bolshevik rule. It was as if Lenin's comment of 8 March 1921 was absolutely correct, 'the last of the hostile armies has been driven from our territory'.

But if the 'hostile armies' had been vanquished, the guerrilla bands remained, posing a widespread threat to Bolshevik rule. In European Russia the major episode was the Tambov Uprising which began on 19 August 1920. The province of Tambov, some 400km south-east of Moscow, was a heavily wooded, densely populated region that produced barely enough food for its increasingly restive inhabitants. Before 1914 it was a haven for outlaws and following the revolutions of 1917 its wildernesses had hosted innumerable deserters, both Red and White. However, Denikin's march on Moscow and subsequent retreat had devastated the area. With the return of Bolshevik food-requisitioning parties in 1920 unrest tipped over into uprising. This was led by A. S. Antonov, a local Left SR with an almost encyclopaedic knowledge of the province's terrain, which, when combined with his flair for leadership and daring tactical style, endeared him to his followers in the manner of a latter-day Robin Hood.

It was the disarming of a Bolshevik grain-requisitioning squad by the people of Khitrova village, followed by the imposition of martial law to cow the locals into submission, that sparked off the uprising. However, until the end of the Polish War and the defeat of Wrangel Trotsky had few men to spare for what Moscow regarded as simple peasant unrest. During the autumn of 1920 Antonov's army of partisans grew, swelling its ranks with Red Army deserters and discontented peasants, encouraged by his call for elections to a new Constituent Assembly, to some 40,000. Despite his actions having been condemned by the local and national SR Party organizations, Antonov disregarded them, running rings around the less mobile Red Army forces in the province. By the beginning of 1921 Lenin had been provoked into demanding the 'swift and complete elimination' of the rebels. Now able to turn the full resources of the Red Army on to Antonov, Trotsky's actions were as ruthless as those of the rebels. Both sides committed horrific atrocities, including amputations, mutilations, crucifixions, disembowelling and other such equally cruel torments. Hostages were taken and slaughtered when demands went unheeded. But despite everything food did not flow into the cities, but nor did Antonov's forces link up with Makhno or similar insurgent groups in the Don region.

In May 1921 Tukhachevsky was given command of some 40,000 Red troops backed by armoured cars, trains and some 60 pieces of artillery. This powerful force was not enough to crush the movement. But when combined with the recently introduced New Economic Policy (NEP) that Lenin had announced on 21 March 1921, things began to change, albeit gradually. The NEP was a pragmatic answer to the critical food shortage that was turning Bolshevik Russia into a famine-stricken wasteland and creating unrest in the cities. In simple terms peasants were allowed to sell their food surplus freely and buy much-needed consumer goods, such as matches, food and fuel. As part of Lenin's NEP, which he intended 'to restore, consolidate and improve peasant farming', the Tambov 'bandits' were offered a final opportunity of amnesty. Gradually, the combination of carrot and stick began to undermine Antonov's support base as the peasants, totally exhausted by war and increasingly apathetic towards any disturbance, began to refuse him sanctuary and supplies. With the coming of summer men slipped away from Antonov's ranks to gather in their harvests which they were now allowed to use for trade. Nevertheless, Antonov and a hard core of supporters fought on in an increasingly hostile environment. Little is known of his last year, but Soviet sources credit the newly re-branded Cheka, the GPU (Glavnoe Politicheskoye Upravlenie), with his death on 29 July 1922. Indeed, *Pravda* announced an end to peasant 'banditry' in late 1922.

Antonov's had not been the only Green, peasant uprising in the wake of the White collapse. Similar events had broken out in 1920–1922 in Siberia, on the Volga and in Central Asia. However, the latter were more nationalist in their aspirations. Late in 1916 the Moslem tribes of Central Asia had begun a guerrilla war against Tsarist mobilization demands that forced them into labour battalions. This rumbled on until 1918 when the demands of food-requisitioning units as usual upset the locals. Despite providing sops to the Moslems by improving their local influence over events at the expense of Russian settlers, various groups sprang up determined to rid the area of Russians of whatever shade of political colouring and re-establish the pre-tsarist states, such as the Emirate of Bukhara. However, given the region's relative isolation, the deserts and the mountainous landscape it took the Red Army, operating slowly along the few railway lines, until 1922 to subdue the major insurgent groups. The last rumblings of discontent were only silenced in the mid-1930s. Once again, it was a combination of carrot and stick that eroded the Basmachi's foundations. Of equal importance was the exploitation of tribal rivalries. From 1920 into 1923 the Red Army had to deploy roughly 150,000 men that fought literally running battles with small groups of Basmachi.

With the internal, provincial uprisings in hand there remained one major problem for the Moscow regime to deal with early in 1921. In many respects it was one that could be thought of as a cannibalistic tragedy in which the revolution consumed its own, the Kronstadt Uprising.

At the heart of the 1917 revolutions were the men of the Baltic Sea Fleet based at the island fortress of Kronstadt, some 30km from Petrograd. They were highly politicized, militant supporters of Lenin's aim of world revolution. However, by mid-1920 the sailors were becoming increasingly disillusioned with the brutal realities of Bolshevik rule, which they had done so much to support for almost three blood-soaked years. Garrisoned by 20,000 men, Kronstadt naval base had provided thousands of foot soldiers for all theatres of the civil war. Replacements to man and maintain the ships, forts and batteries at Kronstadt had come mainly from the countryside and brought with them tales of Bolshevik food requisitioning and other hardships and graft that the revolution claimed to have ended. Such tales added to the indignation many sailors felt at the arrogant and elitist manner and behaviours they saw amongst the Bolshevik bureaucrats and the growing band of commissars. Indeed, some of the more outspoken dubbed the system the 'commissarocracy', drawing parallels with the Romanov autocracy. Again, it was to be a local event, in Petrograd, that sparked off armed insurrection. The first sign of serious unrest was the massive increase in the number of desertions, upwards of 500 in January 1921 alone. Throughout that month the living conditions of the workers in Petrograd had deteriorated alarmingly, buildings were demolished to provide fuel, rations fell below subsistence level and consequently labour unrest increased, as did the repressive methods of the city's Cheka. Martial law was declared on 24 February and rumours of Cheka brutality reached the sailors, who were outraged. Bolshevik censorship denied them access to news and when a delegation of sailors was refused entry to the city the storm broke.

Under the leadership of a petty officer named Petrichenko, a crewman of the battleship *Petropavlovsk*, a committee was formed that drew up a list of reforms. They demanded the Bolsheviks provide a democratic government with freedom of expression. To both Lenin and Trotsky this signalled counter-revolution. Attempts at conciliation failed and when another delegation of sailors 'disappeared' en route to Petrograd, coupled with rumours of troops being sent from the city to restore order in the Baltic Fleet, events and emotions spiralled out of control. Petrichenko and his committee prepared to fight for what they called 'the third revolution of working men and women'.

Although the sailors numbered but 15,000, their position was strong. The guns of the fleet and shore batteries along with scores of machine guns could sweep the frozen waters that the attackers would have to cross. Then when the thaw, daily expected, came who knew what would happen? Indeed, the sailors anticipated revolts all over the RSFSR if only they could hold out until the ice melted.

Tukhachevsky was appointed to lead the reduction of the Kronstadt garrison and assembled the best troops he could along with strong artillery and aerial support. The attacks across the ice were to be led by units of officer cadets, Kursanty, supported by formations that included large numbers of Bolshevik Party members in their ranks.

At the narrowest attack point of 7.5km, the first assault was launched on 7 March. Advancing across the open ice, the Red Army men were slaughtered. Wave after wave was mown down until the attack was called off. Heavily reinforced, Tukhachevsky ordered his men into action again on 10 and 12 March only to increase the tally of dead. As the attackers' morale began to waver, Cheka blocking detachments were placed behind the lines to shoot down any who refused to advance. It was only the news of the introduction of the NEP that led to a dramatic turnaround in events. Almost overnight demoralized Red Army units were motivated to attack again. On 17 March, with the ice melting under their boots, the Kursanty attacked once more, this time from three different directions. Despite taking grievous casualties, they overwhelmed the sailors' lines and broke into Kronstadt town. Just before midnight the Petropavlovsk was captured and the sailors broke. Over 7,000 fled across the still-frozen sea to neutral Finland. Those that were captured faced imprisonment or execution. The 10-day Battle of Kronstadt, the last set-piece battle between technically similar forces during the civil war, cost the Red Army some 10,000 casualties.

Casualty calculation for the Russian Civil War is complicated to say the least. The dead from the war, the epidemics, the 'terrors' and the famines of 1921–1922 has been estimated at anywhere between 8 and 13 million, just under 10 per cent of Russia's population in 1914. Lenin and the Bolsheviks had triumphed but at what a cost in blood. Now they had to build their 'Workers' Paradise' amidst the ruins of a once prosperous nation. It would be many decades before that dream even approached reality. In exile across the globe Greens, Whites, Nationalists and Blacks could only look on and dream what might have been.

Life in independent Georgia had continued much as normal as the civil war raged on across Russia. Here the funeral of a member of the local aristocracy proceeds through the streets of Tiflis.

Ordinary peasant farmers such as this family were continually at the mercy of all sides during the civil war. Their food was essential to the continuation of the conflict. When they finally snapped and rose against the Bolsheviks it was too late to effect change.

Sailors of the Kronstadt naval base check the papers of a civilian in the time before they rose up against what they regarded as a betrayal of the revolution.

A Red Army armoured car patrols the streets of Kronstadt in the days following the suppression of the sailors' uprising.

Red Army commanders with a group of tribal dignitaries during the Basmachi Rebellion. By a combination of carrot and ruthless stick the region was recovered and subject to decades of Russian domination.

Tanks supplied by the British and captured from the Whites provided the nucleus for the Red Army's first armoured units in the early 1920s.

General A. P. Kutepov, commander of I Army Corps under Wrangel in 1920 and veteran of the Ice March in 1918, encouraged anti-Bolshevism from exile. He was kidnapped by the Soviets in 1930 and died en route to Russia.

Wrangel and his staff pause whilst discussing welfare and mutual support for veterans, Belgrade. During the 1920s, Belgrade, Yugoslavia, was home to many Russian Army exiles of all ranks.

Major General A. V Turkul, commander of the Drozdovsky Infantry Division under Wrangel, who lost three brothers during the civil war. During the Second World War he actively supported the anti-Soviet Vlasov movement.

During the autumn of 1919 Denikin and his deputy Lieutenant General I. P. Romanovsky (right rear of car) were losing their popularity. However, it was Romanovsky that bore the brunt of the AFSR's hatred and blame for the failure of the Moscow Campaign. Romanovsky was murdered by a VA officer in Istanbul on 5 April 1920.

J. V. Stalin, pictured here at the height of his power in 1945, cut his military and political teeth during the civil war. During this time he established close relations with Buddeny and Voroshilov who both rose to the rank of Marshals of the Soviet Union during Stalin's reign.

Marshal of the Soviet Union G. K. Zhukov, a cavalryman in the Tsar's army, joined 1st Moscow Cavalry Division of the Red Army. He fought on various fronts and received the Order of the Red Banner for his part in the suppression of the Tambov Uprising.

Marshal of the Soviet Union K. K. Rokossovsky, politically active in the Tsarist army whilst he served in the cavalry. He fought against Kolchak and later Baron Ungern-Sternberg as the commander of a cavalry regiment.

When the Russian Civil War ended a sort of calm descended on the steppes, villages and cities. But for years afterwards disease and famine stalked the unhappy land that was the USSR and then came the Second World War.

Armoured trains and cavalry provided both flank cover and spearheads for armies on both sides where the fronts were little more than lines on a map. This armoured train, the 'General Shkuro', is one belonging to the AFSR.

It was the infantry that bore the brunt of the fighting. On foot, on country carts or on trains, they were moved hither and thither to participate in actions that bore more resemblance to the encounter battles of earlier times than the trenches and wire of the First World War.

Air power was increasing in importance during the First World War and continued to do so during the Russian Civil War. Ground attack, reconnaissance and supply flights as well as plane-to-plane dog fights all featured throughout the period.

Dead White infantry on the barbed wire of the Kakhovka Bridgehead. This battle of attrition showcased the defensive network that the Red Army would use to such effect at the watershed Battle of Kursk in 1943. Such engagements were untypical of the battles of the civil war where, generally, small forces fought little battles with their flanks in the air.